WARMED by HOPE

How Divine Power Shaped This Man's Story

By

Ron Nickerson

TEACH Services, Inc.
P U B L I S H I N G
www.TEACHServices.com • (800) 367-1844

World rights reserved. This book or any portion thereof may not be copied or reproduced in any form or manner whatever, except as provided by law, without the written permission of the publisher, except by a reviewer who may quote brief passages in a review.

The author assumes full responsibility for the accuracy of all facts and quotations as cited in this book. The opinions expressed in this book are the author's personal views and interpretations, and do not necessarily reflect those of the publisher.

This book is provided with the understanding that the publisher is not engaged in giving spiritual, legal, medical, or other professional advice. If authoritative advice is needed, the reader should seek the counsel of a competent professional.

Copyright © 2025 Ron Nickerson
Copyright © 2025 TEACH Services, Inc.
ISBN-13: 978-1-4796-1791-3 (Paperback)
ISBN-13: 978-1-4796-1792-0 (ePub)
Library of Congress Control Number: 2024926304

All scripture quotations, unless otherwise indicated, are taken from the New King James Version®. Copyright © 1982 by Thomas Nelson. Used by permission. All rights reserved.

DEDICATION

My father was a storyteller, and his story-based approach to life went as far back as I can remember. Our lives were blessed by this love of his. Influenced by my father, I have also always been a storyteller; first to my children, and then to anyone who would lend an ear.

Stories! What is it about them? For every one that is told, there are at least three different versions. First there is the storyteller's account, based on his understanding of what happened. Next is the story that each person hears, which, although it is the same tale, is based on *their* experiences. Finally, there are the actual facts.

I do not propose that the stories in this book are anything more than my recollection of events (or those of my father as he recounted events to me). One almost needs to offer a disclaimer: "The scenes depicted here may or may not reflect the actual events." However, though they may seem fictitious to some, these stories are based on fact. True, they are *my* facts, but to paraphrase a character in *A Knight's Tale*, "These are my words, and are thus beyond contestation!" Still, storytelling must have a purpose. In my view, it must communicate a message … and there is no greater message today than that of Jesus Christ.

One life is not necessarily blessed over another. The stories one chooses to relate do not depict all the lows. In fact, each of our lives is a collection of highs and lows. There have been many things in my life I wish had never happened, but God has been tremendously gracious in forgiving me. He can use you, too, no matter what is in your past. Mercy flows freely from His throne.

It is thus my purpose to help people young and old to connect with Christ's Word. Every story will start with a Scripture, since the purpose of all Scripture is to draw closer to Christ. If my stories help just one person connect with the Bible verses provided in this book, then I have succeeded.

All of the stories which follow have, at one time or another, been a part of my sermons. I never expected to be writing them down, but for years my loving wife has been encouraging me to do just that so that I can pass them on. In fact, there are many people who have encouraged me over the years to begin this project; it would be impossible to list them all.

That being said, I must acknowledge my wife, Lorelei, for her constant encouragement, and Ellen Busl for her hours of correcting and smoothing my crude attempts to convert oral English into the written word. This is my first attempt at writing, and it is surprising how different written language is from spoken language. Without their efforts this project would have been doomed before it started.

Lastly, because of my father's influence on my life through his storytelling, I dedicate this collection of stories in loving memory of Robert Leon Nickerson, Sr.

TABLE OF CONTENTS

Chapter 1: Nantucket: The Beginning (Prov. 16:9) 9

Chapter 2: Harbor Buoys (Exod. 20:12) 15

Chapter 3: Eaton's Neck Light (1 John 5:11, 12). 20

Chapter 4: Food by Prayer (Matt. 6:1-4) 25

Chapter 5: Reconnecting (John 15:5) 29

Chapter 6: Captain B. (Heb. 13:1, 2) 33

Chapter 7: Crew Abuse (Rom. 5:3, 4) 37

Chapter 8: False Charges (Rom. 8:28). 41

Chapter 9: Water in the Waveguide (Rom. 12:16) 47

Chapter 10: First Real Duty (Phil. 2:14, 15) 51

Chapter 11: Boot Camp (Phil. 1:6). 56

Chapter 12: Eye of the Storm (Ps. 91:11).........................60

Chapter 13: No Lifeboat? (Ps. 86:6, 7)...........................66

Chapter 14: The Keo (John 10:27) 69

Chapter 15: Simus Kudirka (Rom. 12:3)..........................72

Chapter 16: Holly and the Door (Ps. 91:11) 82

Chapter 17: Transfer to Alaska (Ps. 37:37-40) 84

Chapter 18: Cold is a State of Mind (Ps. 46:1-3) 94

Chapter 19: Thomas (Matt. 7:1, 2)..............................102

Chapter 20: The Tow Line (1 Peter 4:7).........................109

Chapter 21: Spiders! (Josh. 24:14, 15) 113

Chapter 22: The Tower (John 3:14-16) 118

Chapter 23: Muttley (Heb. 12:6)................................122

Chapter 24: Missionary's Faith (Hab. 2:4).......................125

Chapter 25: Engineer John (Prov. 3:5, 6).......................130

Chapter 26: Anechoic Chamber (Mark 15:34)...................137

Chapter 27: The Sheep Story (John 10:27) 140

Chapter 28: Whoopi and the Swamp (Matt. 18:12-14)...........143

Chapter 29: Emma and the Bear (1 Peter 5:8) 147

Chapter 30: Lost Without Knowledge (2 Tim. 3:16, 17).........150

Chapter 31: High Water (Ps. 91:11)............................154

Chapter 32: King Cobra! (Ps. 91:13-16) 158

Chapter 33: Ohio Road Trip (Prov. 3:1, 2) 161

Chapter 34: Shot Across the Bow (Titus 2:11, 12) 164

Chapter 35: Prayer Is the Answer (Titus 2:13) 171

Chapter 36: Hydrogen (John 3:8) 174

Chapter 37: Trains and Trestles (Prov. 16:25) 177

Chapter 38: State of the Dead (Job 27:2-6) 180

Chapter 39: Cancer Again (Micah 6:8) 186

Chapter 40: Pastor Finally (Matt. 6:33) 191

Chapter 41: Seeing a Miracle (Matt. 21:22) 196

Chapter 42: Speaking the Word (Matt. 10:19, 20) 200

Chapter 43: Age vs Mission (Matt. 10:32) 203

Chapter 44: Evangelistic Series (Matt. 28:18-20a) 206

Chapter 45: Trust (Prov. 3:5, 6) 209

Chapter 46: Kiss (1 John 5:11, 12) 213

Bibliography 217

CHAPTER 1: NANTUCKET: THE BEGINNING

A man's heart plans his ways, but the Lord directs his steps. (Prov. 16:9)

I guess there's no better way to begin than at the beginning, or at least my beginning. It was October 31, 1948, and I had just become the third of what were to be six Nickerson children, most of which, like me, were born on Nantucket Island.

There is a small cottage hospital on that island. Like all small cottage hospitals, it is unfortunately limited in comparison to a major metropolitan medical facility. And I had just been born with a serious condition that caused seizures so frequent that the island's doctors concluded that if I was not taken to Boston Children's Hospital within the next week, I would surely die.

How do you tell a parent that the only hope for their child's survival lies beyond their reach? Nantucket is, after all, accessible only by boat or plane, and this was a time before the wonders of radar and GPS. People were at the mercy of the weather; weather like that on this frosty, foggy, and strange Halloween.

If you have ever been on an island, it will not have taken you long to understand that fog is a part of island life. Some love it, some hate it, all have to deal with it; and at that time, weather was just something that *happened* with little forewarning. It may be hard for young people today to understand the chances that were taken without knowing the forecast, but our "forecasts" depended more upon empirical evidence than the computer models and satellite images we are used to today.

For my parents, the question remained: how to get me to the mainland? In the words of Booker T. Washington, "Success is to be measured not so much by the position that one has reached in life as by the obstacles which he has overcome while trying to succeed." To my father, Bob, failure was not an option.

God needed to show him that faith was a stronger force than willful determination, but at the time, to my father, God was a last resort, not a first line of defense. *Wasn't religion mainly for the women?* he would think. *Doesn't God want us to direct our own steps? To make our own plans, and when we get in trouble, call on Him?* That day my father decided to do what he had always done: analyze the situation and devise a plan.

Issue one: how to go? The last person to walk on water had left nearly 2,000 years ago, and getting off the island by boat was not only more dangerous than flying but also more difficult; thus he crossed it off his list. That left one approach: airplane. My father was, after all, a pilot, and he had a small Piper Cub. The only rub was that the Nantucket airport was not allowing any flights inbound or off the island.

The second issue was: who would go with him? This trip had a lot of risks, and my mother was in no condition to fly, not to mention that she might simply not go along with his plan. After all, flying in the blind with just a compass was difficult at best. This was compounded by the fact that if he flew off course by just a few degrees, they'd never reach any destination and wind up running out of fuel over an angry ocean. He finally decided my mother's brother, also named Bob, would come.

Chapter 1: Nantucket: The Beginning

When the plan was presented to my mother, there must have been a good deal of discussion, but in the end they could see no other option. She met with the newly-formed company of believers to ask God to intercede on our behalf.

Once again my father could not see the need to consult an all-loving God. Didn't He expect us to do what we could, and then He'd fill in the gaps? (He hadn't yet learned that the Lord directs our steps according to the Bible!) Rather than waste precious time on his knees, my father and his brother-in-law went to Nantucket airport.

The fog was so thick that you could cut it with a knife. Visibility was measured in feet, not yards, and the forecast offered no relief. How could they take off? Realizing that to even ask was hopeless, they opted for trickery.

They sought permission to test the plane by taxiing back and forth on the runway. Unaware of the situation my family faced and seeing nothing wrong with the inquiry, the airport gave their permission to proceed. Step one was now a go!

After a couple of runs up and down the runway, they reached the point of no return. Bob looked at Bob and said, "This is it: it's all or nothing." My uncle Bob had wrapped me in a blanket and was holding me out away from his body, because my seizures were getting closer and closer together. I was becoming harder and harder to hold on to. My father watched my struggling uncle and said, "This had better work, or none of us will be home tonight."

The truth of the matter was that even if it worked, they probably would not be *allowed* to return. Full throttle, they headed down the runway, and before the tower knew what was happening, they took off.

Unable to see anything, my dad climbed as quickly as possible until finally they were above the clouds. He set his course for the general direction of New Bedford, checked his airspeed, and calculated how long it would take until they'd be over land once again. Then they settled in for his calculated flight time.

The broadcast radio talked about there being fog even over the mainland, but they assumed that it was probably patchy. The one beauty of a Piper Cub is that if there is an even halfway-decently-sized field, you can put it down and survive. So that was the last part of the plan: fly until you can see an open field, and put it down.

Flying by compass is not as easy as it sounds. A little turbulence, a little shifting to the left or to the right, and the compass starts moving back and forth forty degrees to either side. I have never flown a plane, yet I know what it's like to try to steer by compass at sea: if you stare at the compass, your vessel will be all over the place. The only way to truly steer by compass is to pick an object in the distance and focus on that; then you can maintain your course.

Of course in the air there are no objects. I don't have a clue as to how they could have succeeded … and I don't think my father did, either.

More than the allotted time to reach New Bedford passed. Still my dad and uncle could see nothing but beautifully billowing clouds. They had no idea where they were in that white maze. *So what now?* he must have thought. *You can't go back, and you can't go forward.*

There was only one logical choice: he started circling where he was. Just maybe, a hole would open in the clouds, and they would then be able to see an area large enough to land.

> *With sweating hands gripping the yoke and nowhere else to turn, he started to pray.*

There were two problems with that conclusion. One, running up and down the runway on Nantucket, along with the trip across Buzzards Bay, had eaten up a good share of their gas supply. Two, if an opening did not develop soon, any attempt to land would undoubtedly mean death.

Seeing Uncle Bob continue to struggle to hold onto me didn't help the situation. My father was now faced with a no-win situation for his new son, his dear friend, and himself. With sweating hands gripping the yoke and nowhere else to turn, he started to pray.

"Dear God, it seems I've never asked anything of You before. I would not be surprised if You didn't listen to me now. In a short time, I'm going to have to put this plane down, and I have no clue as to where I am. I realize now that I should have reached out to You before this. But if You can find it in Your will to spare my son, my brother-in-law, and me, I will forever be in Your debt."

As he finished the prayer, he realized there was virtually no fuel left. At the same moment, Uncle Bob spotted an opening in the clouds. "To your right at 3 o'clock," he said. "I think I see a road!"

Chapter 1: Nantucket: The Beginning

Banking to the right, my father also saw the small opening. Yes! It did appear to be a paved road. But were there power lines? Cars coming? Was it an intersection? With no time to second-guess, he dove the plane into the hole. As the wheels touched down, the sky closed like a trap door.

While he slowed the plane, they realized that the road was wider than normal. More importantly, there were no power lines or traffic. Rolling forward, they soon realized why: the pavement they had landed on was a runway at New Bedford airport! In fact, they were the only plane to take off that day from Nantucket airport, and the only one to land in New Bedford.

Yet the journey was not over. They had to get to Boston Children's Hospital as soon as possible. At the airport they rented a taxi to take them to Boston. This time they prayed before leaving: "God, You have shown us we are in Your hands, so now we ask You to guide us the rest of the way. We leave it up to You."

Two miles from the airport, the taxi broke down; but now they knew that God could do anything. Just as they rolled to a stop, a Massachusetts state trooper pulled up behind them. Once he learned of their situation, they transferred to his patrol car. With sirens blaring and lights flashing, they completed the journey in half the time it would have taken.

I started the story with a text from Proverbs. The gist of it is that God directs our steps. The day of my birth, I could make no plans and I could not take steps, but God was in control.

Many years later my mother wrote me a note that I have carried in my wallet since 1991, when I graduated from Fitchburg State University. It reads, *Dear Ronnie, I knew when you won the battle over death in the first months of your life you were going to succeed in whatever you undertook, and in the process you make me very proud. -Mom*

When my father passed away in 2001, my mother gave me a handwritten book of his sermons that he had wanted me to have. In that book he wrote, *Hope is a power, encouraged and strengthened by faith, lays hold upon future realities, standing upon the sure promises of God and inspired with the certainty of future possessions.* I now have this written in the front of my Bible and refer to it often. I have no idea where these words first originated from, but they have changed my life.

In this life we can plan, we can think, and we may even know where we should go; but in the end, we need to realize that God has a plan and that He directs our steps.

CHAPTER 2: HARBOR BUOYS

Honor your father and your mother, that your days may be long upon the land which the Lord your God is giving you. (Exod. 20:12)

I can remember being told many crazy things as a child. Perhaps the craziest was that when you did something wrong or went where you shouldn't, your guardian angel would leave you to your own devices. I know now that when Jesus tells us that He will never leave us nor forsake us, He means exactly that.

This is not meant to be an encouragement to sin. As Paul stated in Romans chapter 6, verses 1 and 2, "What shall we say then? Shall we continue in sin that grace may abound? Certainly not!"

Our desire to do what is right comes from God, and our power to overcome also comes from God. With Him all things are possible; on top of that, in John chapter 15, verse 5, we are told that without Jesus we can do nothing. It becomes clear where the doing comes from.

This story shows how God not only directs our steps but also those of others to complete His tasks.

It was summer, and it was hot; and what does every young kid raised by the ocean want to do on a hot summer day in July? Go to the beach and have fun with lots of cousins and friends!

Fort Phoenix in Fairhaven was one of our favorite spots. There were rocks to climb, cannons to pretend to shoot, and the beach to enjoy. As far as I was concerned, there was only one thing that could ruin a day like this.

Then I heard those terrible and ominous words from my mother: "Ronnie, it's your turn to watch your younger brother. I want you to stay on the rocks and be sure that he is safe."

> *Oh, why do we wait until we see no way out before seeking heavenly guidance from an all-loving God?*

Why is it when a ten-year-old is asked to do the responsible thing, he feels he is being persecuted? It is funny that as a parent, when my own children have confronted me with the statement, "It's not fair," I have responded, "Life is not fair … deal with it." That answer is cheap comfort, and it was separated by too many years from the little boy who was told to watch his brother. To see my brothers, sisters, and cousins head for the water while I stayed behind seemed so unjust.

At that time in history, the dike in New Bedford Harbor did not exist. In its place were a number of buoys designating the entrance to the channel (and thus into the harbor). Though technically illegal, one of the most exciting things to do was to swim to one of those buoys and use it like a diving platform. Those buoys were beyond the view of the general beach area and thus out of sight of our parents. This made the challenge even more exciting!

Yet here I sat on the rocks with my brother, watching the fun that the other kids were having.

Chapter 2: Harbor Buoys

It is no coincidence that the idea to disobey comes along with all of the justifications for your goal. I convinced myself that disobeying would be okay if they never found out; that all I really wanted was to have just one dive off the buoy, and then I would be satisfied. But honoring your mother and your father does not come with exceptions. It means just that: to honor your father and mother. Dishonest action always has a price.

I turned to my brother and tried to set down ground rules to justify my action. "Your job is to stay here on the rocks for just a few minutes while I swim to the buoy and back." Why did I think he would obey me if I didn't obey our parents?

Slipping into the water while giving my brother the sign to *stay* like an obedient dog, I headed for the buoy. Three quarters of the way there, I saw my cousin signaling me to turn around. Flipping over and treading water, I saw why. My little brother was halfway between me and the shore, trying desperately to keep up.

The current in New Bedford harbor can be quite powerful. It is definitely too powerful for the swimming skills of a six-year-old. It was quite evident not only that was he not gaining on me but also that he was being carried out toward Buzzards Bay.

Realizing that I had made a mistake that might cost my brother his life, I turned around. In the meantime my cousin jumped off the buoy and swam as fast as she could to reach him.

We both reached my brother at about the same time and tried to pull him toward shore, but despite all our efforts, land was getting further and further away instead of closer and closer! Panic started to set in. We stopped, and while treading water we tried to figure what could be done.

My cousin suggested that one of us should float on our back to act like a life preserver for my brother, while the other tried to pull toward shore. When the one who was pulling got tired, we could change places.

Before you say it, I know the logic was slightly flawed. Hadn't we already failed to pull him to shore together? Instead of being a solution, this new strategy seemed to make matters worse. Soon we began to realize that even if we let him go, we might have trouble making it back to shore ourselves.

I feared that God would not listen to me because I was in a state of disobedience to my parents, yet I prayed anyway. Oh, why do we wait until we see no way out before seeking heavenly guidance from an all-loving God? What will it take to help us understand that seeking God first is always the best approach?

It's amazing how a child in desperation will say anything to make a prayer more appealing to God, when all God asks of us is to trust and obey. Today as I look back at that prayer, I smile at what I promised: to dedicate my life to God's service if He found a way to save us. It took forty-five years to fulfill that promise!

Meanwhile the people on the beach now seemed like small dots. It does seem amazing how God often waits until we are at the end of our rope before pulling us in. Perhaps it's to remind us that if we seek Him first, we can avoid being in these predicaments. As I've gone through life, I have realized that God has often had to hit me alongside the head with a two-by-four to get me to follow the path that He chose for my life. In that moment, despite reeling from that two-by-four blow, the prayer gave me hope (remember: *hope is a power encouraged and strengthened by faith*).

Then, out of what seemed like nowhere, we heard a voice behind us: "What in the world are you kids doing out here this far from shore?"

It was a man in a small boat, reaching for three kids in trouble. Pulling us in, he asked us where we came from. Though it was hard to talk while shivering with fear, we told him Fort Phoenix. Shaking his head, he redirected his boat. "I can get you close enough to the beach for you to safely get ashore."

As we got closer and closer, the people on shore (who by this time were trying to spot us) recognized that we were being brought to safety. Once the boat was as close to shore as possible, they helped us over the side to finish the journey.

I've never been so happy and at the same time so afraid to see my mother. With tears in her eyes, she scooped up my brother and me and drowned us in kisses.

I was never punished for my disobedience, and I cannot say that I never again disobeyed (I was, after all, a ten-year-old boy), but I did learn from the events of that day.

All our decisions come with consequences; some good and some bad. The guidelines that God has given us, otherwise called the Ten Commandments, are not about dos and don'ts; they are about leading us down the path that God has chosen for us. And honoring our mothers and our fathers is not about avoiding consequences but rather about understanding what our relationship ought to be to our Heavenly Father.

CHAPTER 3: EATON'S NECK LIGHT

And this is the testimony: that God has given us eternal life, and this life is in His Son. He who has the Son has life; he who does not have the Son of God does not have life. (1 John 5:11, 12)

There is probably no text in the Bible that better explains the Gospel than this one. It is all broken down into knowing one person: Jesus Christ. I remember studying karate with my daughter and having the sensei tell us over and over to focus. He was of course correct, with the exception that the key was not focusing on ourselves but instead focusing on Christ.

There are many who make obedience their idol and try with all their own will to do what is right. But to paraphrase Pastor Lee Venden, it is not what you do that matters but who you know, because who you know changes what you do.

Chapter 3: Eaton's Neck Light

As a chief petty officer in the United States Coast Guard, one of my duties at Station Eaton's Neck was to be the weekend duty officer for a lifeboat station. My responsibilities included directing the search and rescue operations, which required that I maintain proficiency in the operation of small boats. In order to do so, I would periodically direct the rescue operation as the crew chief (it is only by manning a boat that we can understand its limitations and abilities).

The command post was located on a hill about fifty yards from the docks. The ready crew leader (the crew leader who would receive the next call) stayed in close proximity to the command post, while the crew themselves needed to be either in the designated area near the pier, on the boat, or close enough to respond the minute the station siren went off. Not surprisingly, the average response time to get a boat underway was about one and a half minutes, and that included the duty coxswain getting to the boat with the destination information.

One Saturday in August, a distress call came in midafternoon. There was a chance of squalls, but it appeared to be a bright day. Let's face it, the weatherman is wrong more than we'd like to admit; and with that in mind, I picked this call to head out with the crew.

A Coast Guard rescue crew is like a well-oiled machine: four men who act, think, and work as one. Each man is trained in all aspects of small boat operation. The first one to reach the boat starts the engines, the second goes for the bow line, and the third releases the stern line. It is amazing how these steps occur simultaneously; it is a credit to the efficiency of these life-saving crews. Meanwhile, the lead crew member gathers the information about the destination. As the boat moves forward past the end of the dock, he jumps from the pier to the deck in one fluid motion.

Like I said, the total elapsed time from alarm to underway was less than two minutes.

The lead crew member on this call remained in the command post. Having decided to accompany them, I jumped to the deck of the forty-foot rescue boat and made my way to the helm to take control. Less than one and a half hours later, we had the disabled vessel in tow and were headed for Port Jefferson Harbor. Once the vessel was safely secured in port, it was time to return to the base and prepare for the next call.

Besides periodically honing my own skills, it was necessary to use every opportunity to train the others. In view of that I took this opportunity to give some coxswain training to one of the newest members of the crew, young Seaman Bill. Bill was a little wet behind the ears. Being new to this group, he needed to build not only his skills but also his confidence.

The sky was getting a little dark, but it did not appear that it was going to be a problem on the short trip back to the base. I, on the other hand, had been up since Friday morning and was starting to feel the effects of so little sleep. A forty-foot rescue boat is a good-sized craft and has two bunks in the living area below deck. I decided it was the perfect place to catch a quick nap while also testing the confidence of Seaman Bill.

Years at sea and my general constitution have enabled me to catch a quick nap almost anywhere. I have even been known to fall asleep standing up. I'm not sure whether this is a boon or a curse. Regardless, I must've been out as soon as my head hit the pillow, for the next thing I remember was hearing somebody yell, "Chief!"

Upon opening my eyes, I realized I was looking sideways at the top of the table. This would not have been a bad thing were it not for the fact that the table was two feet taller than the bed! By the time my body came back down and reconnected with the bed, my feet were already moving. At the cabin door I was met by wind, rain, and at least forty-foot seas.

Forty-foot waves while in a forty-foot boat is not a pleasant situation. Have you ever seen a small child swing his legs left and right in a bathtub? What happens to the shallow water of the tub? Now you can understand what Long Island Sound is like with high winds. I could tell by the look on Seaman Bill's face that he was petrified.

Behind the helm there was a web screen designed to keep the coxswain from being swept away. Attached to that screen were belts allowing you to secure yourself in the event that a boat did, in fact, capsize (these boats were designed to self-right if they rolled, but that wouldn't help if you were not still attached to it).

As I secured myself to the screen I noticed that the radar was no longer working. Turning to one of the crew, I signaled my surprise. He yelled, "It went out about ten minutes ago!" Reaching for the microphone, I discovered that the radio was also not working.

"What else is not working?" I yelled above the storm, only to see them point to where the lifeboat used to be.

As they held on for dear life, I fought to make our way back to the safety of the base. The sky was dark, and visibility decreased with each pounding wave. We wondered if we were going to test this boat's ability to self-right.

Eaton's Neck Light was situated on a cliff high above the harbor entrance. My family and my home were directly behind the lighthouse. But one more major obstacle was in our path: the rocks surrounding the entrance to Eaton's Neck Harbor.

> "What else is not working?" I yelled above the storm, only to see them point to where the lifeboat used to be.

In weather this severe, the harbor buoys were next to useless. Wind, waves, and poor visibility made relying on those buoys to guide us into the harbor almost impossible. I decided that all hands had to watch instead for the rocky areas.

I turned to young Seaman Bill. He knew what he had to do without a word being said. He made his way to the bow and secured himself to the railing. With each wave the bow of the boat went under the water, and he would be able to see how close we were to those rocks. Each time the bow came up he let out the breath he was holding and either yelled "Rocks!" or "Clear!" so that we could proceed.

It seemed that every time we got close to the entrance, more rocks appeared, and we had to swing around and approach again. Each time it took ten to fifteen minutes to swing around and return to the entrance buoy to begin another approach.

Besides having a high order Fresnel lens, the light on Eaton's Neck was shaded on the back side to prevent it from being seen over land. Also, on either side it was red, so that you could only see the white light if you were on the correct approach to the harbor entrance.

Remembering this, I started to watch for that white light. As we got closer, I yelled to the crew to intensify the search for rocks.

Every time we took our eyes off of the light and looked for the rocks, we were sure to find them. Isn't that how it is in life? Whenever we look for trouble, it appears at every turn.

After several failed attempts, I realized that the only way to succeed would be to keep my eyes on the light. This was easier said than done, for every bone in our bodies cried out for us to focus on our troubles. But when all our efforts failed, I determined to focus on the light alone. Not taking my eyes off of it, I kept the light white. A few moments later, we were in the safety of the harbor.

Many will tell us that focusing on Christ is not enough; that you have to do this or you have to do that in order to succeed. The Bible is clear: he who has the Son has life, he who does not have the Son does not have life. Don't let the rocks of life sidetrack you from this fundamental understanding of the Gospel.

Looking for problems will always yield problems. We do not have the power or the skill set to overcome alone, but with God all things are possible. Focusing on Jesus is our part to play as we walk this journey of life.

CHAPTER 4: FOOD BY PRAYER

Take heed that you do not your charitable deeds before men, to be seen by them. Otherwise you have no reward from your Father in heaven. Therefore, when you do a charitable deed, do not sound the trumpet before you as the hypocrites do in the synagogues and in the streets, that they may have glory from men. Assuredly, I say to you, they have their reward. But when you do a charitable deed, do not let your left hand know what your right hand is doing, that your charitable deed may be in secret; and your Father who sees in secret will Himself reward you openly. (Matt. 6:1-4)

In today's society we hear so much about paying it forward, but what exactly is paying it forward? In the truest meaning of the term, no one would know, or want to know, who was paying and what was forwarded.

Our family went through a very tough time when I was about five or six years old. Despite that fact, we children never knew that it was happening; my parents concealed it very well. Life continued, days passed, and we never suspected how hard things had become.

Yes, we were aware that there seemed to be less food and few to no treats, but that in itself set off no alarms; no red flags. We were happy in our own little world, devoid of the stress and anxiety that my parents faced. They sacrificed so that we would not know. I will never know how long they went without so that we children could *have*.

Yet all roads end somewhere, and the end of this road of not knowing finally came. My father called all of the family into the living room. In our day that was the center of activity for everyday life; the place where we shared, loved, laughed, and, yes, truly lived. We knew that something had happened because, unlike his usual, happy self, he was subdued, soft, and purposeful. The tone of his voice always spoke volumes.

As we gathered in a circle, he told us it was a time for prayer; and not family worship but something deeper. He started to pray, "Our heavenly Father, we do not know where our next meal is coming from. We do not know what is going to happen."

I remember asking myself, *What is he talking about?* Then the realization began to sink in: we were out of money and out of food.

My father was an incredibly spiritual person and was always the rock of the family. He knew what it meant to depend on God, so for the next fifteen minutes he pleaded his case.

Then the amazing happened! There was a knock on the door. How is it that when we approach God, He has our answer already in motion; our help already en route?!

At first we all hesitated to move. Pausing, my father went to answer. Standing there in the hallway were some members of our church. In their arms were bags of groceries.

How did they know? Who had called them? Why were they here? Three real and significant questions, and all were explained with the same answer: "A Savior who cares!"

One said, "We were impressed that you might need these groceries. I hope we have not offended you by bringing them."

Chapter 4: Food by Prayer

In a state of shock, my father took the bags and set them on the table. With a shaking voice he said, "I cannot pay you today, but I will as soon as I am able."

One of them looked at my father and told him that he didn't need to pay them back. "But should an opportunity arise," they said, "and you feel that the Lord is speaking, then do the same thing for somebody else. It will be God directing you." With that they all left, and we enjoyed a delicious supper.

The lesson that we learned that day was never forgotten. More than once after that when we went grocery shopping, my father picked up a little extra. He would consider who might be in need and take it to their house.

There were times when we brought groceries to a home, left them on the stoop, and walked away. Other times we stood there and handed them off into open arms. Now they call it paying it forward, but in that day it was called sharing the love.

Now flash forward some sixty years, when I got to hear about the same thing happening again.

My daughter was at university. One day as she was going to a restaurant near her school, there was a man sitting on the sidewalk who was obviously panhandling. Everyone passed him by. At first she was no different, but something made her pause and turn around.

Walking back to the man, she looked down. Of course she had no cash (this is the twenty-first century; instead of metal coins, we have plastic cards). Despite this, the process was the same.

She asked the man if he was hungry. He didn't have to answer; the look on his face said it all. She reached down, lifted him up, and brought him into the restaurant.

"Let him have whatever he wants," she told the clerk. While his sandwich was made, a few young kids in line behind her started to give her a hard time. "You're being used," said one. "He's taking advantage of you!" said another. But she didn't stop, and when the clerk realized what was happening, he added to the order so that the man had a full meal.

As the startled boys looking on, my daughter turned to them and told them, "If God wants me to be used, then I will be used! If God wants me to be the source of this man's meal, then I'll be the source."

Without knowing what had transpired years earlier when I was a child, my daughter had performed a similar act of mercy.

Matthew chapter 25 tells us clearly how Jesus expects us to treat our fellows: not for glory, not for the reward, but because this is the way He would have us behave.

All too often we expect something in return. No matter what we do in this mindset, we will be doing it for the wrong reason. I don't care if it's a Bible study, I don't even care if it's a smile: to do things with the expectation of acceptance, honor, monetary reward, or even for a spiritual reward is to do them for the wrong reason.

Jesus healed people because they were sick. Jesus loved them because they needed loving. Jesus shared because they needed to know that there was and is a way.

CHAPTER 5: RECONNECTING

I am the vine, you *are* the branches. He who abides in Me, and I in him, bears much fruit; for without Me you can do nothing. (John 15:5)

This next story introduces a time in my life when I reconnected with and recommitted to Jesus Christ. We will revisit the larger narrative of this period over the course of several stories, although the sequence of events will be somewhat broken up by other stories and shifts in time. Because there are many parts, there will also be several Bible texts.

The settings are real. And many people will be mentioned, but not by their actual names so as to protect their anonymity. Many of them will forever hold a place in my heart, and I hope to meet them again someday when Christ returns!

I had been off the ship and onshore for almost a year, but some things still had not changed. I had been to church, but at the same time I had not been to church. Have you ever gone for a drive to work or some other familiar place but when you arrive, you are not able to remember how you got there? Life at that time was just like that. I had been going through the motions but was not feeling the feelings. There was something missing; something not there ... but Jesus was going to bring that to an end soon!

It all started soon after I first reported to my new Long Island assignment at Station Eaton's Neck (you, reader, have already seen it, but this was my first time). The lifeboat station was situated at the end of Henry Morgan's estate. Though the primary purpose of the station was search and rescue, my mission was to maintain and repair the automated system which controlled the lighthouses on both sides of Long Island Sound. Of course you never have just one duty in the service, so I also stood command duty at the lifeboat station on weekends.

I was back with my family, and we had a beautiful townhouse at the base of a historic lighthouse, but something was missing; something

Beautiful and historic (and life-saving!) Eaton's Neck Light.

integral to my upbringing: God. Lorelei and I discussed the issue. We had two beautiful daughters who, though still toddlers, needed to experience a relationship with Jesus, so we decided to seek out the nearest Seventh-day Adventist Church. The real truth was that *we* needed this restoration more than either one of us realized.

The nearest church was in the adjoining town. It was an easy twenty-minute drive past beach homes that sat amidst the beauty that constituted Huntington and Northport Long Island. The little church was equally picturesque.

The congregation was directed by a young pastor named Nick who had a passion for Christ. We attended that first Sabbath thinking we could slip in, sit in the back, and quietly leave without being detected (once again, God had other plans). We were warmly welcomed, and we enjoyed the service, but we retreated to our home at the base as fast as we could.

One evening of that first week, Pastor Nick showed up at our door. He was one of these people who you instantly feel connected to; one who has an aura of love floating before and behind them and who is willing to share. The next week he came again, and the next week, and the next week, and the next!

On one of his visits, he asked if I would be interested in starting a Pathfinders club. I had never told him that I had been involved with Pathfinders for many years, but somehow he knew of my background. I had participated from the fifth grade through academy, first in Pathfinders and then in the Medical Cadet Corps (MCC). Even now I can still recall the joy and excitement that it added to my life. But I didn't answer right away, saying I had to think about his request.

After considering, I decided to go forward. There was, however, one caveat: as an active member of the military, I was not supposed to wear another uniform. So I agreed to do it using my Coast Guard uniform. This really wasn't so strange, as both my military uniform and the Pathfinder ones were khaki.

The more I was involved, the more I connected; the more I connected, the more I was involved. Six months later, at the first camporee, I pulled the pastor to one side and asked him a serious question:

"Pastor Nick, when you asked me to lead the Pathfinders, did you know that I was not living the life that I should have been? Did you know that there were things that needed to be corrected in my life for me to be a good representative of the Adventist Church?"

He looked at me and said, "Yes."

I asked why he hadn't said something to me.

He merely said, "Did *you* realize that there were things you needed to correct in your life?"

I answered, "Yes."

"Then why would I need to tell you? My job is to love you and let Jesus do the rest!"

I have never forgotten that to this day. Our lives had started to change during that time without our even realizing a change was happening.

Too often we try to tell people how to live before we tell them Who to live for. Too often we are concerned with what they do rather than with Who they know. But I have found that if you can introduce somebody to Jesus, and show them how to have a relationship with Him, then as they draw closer and closer to our Lord, He will fill in the gaps.

CHAPTER 6: CAPTAIN B.

Let brotherly love continue. Do not forget to entertain strangers, for by so *doing* some have unwittingly entertained angels. (Heb. 13:1, 2)

All men are children of God and should be treated with love and respect. Many times it seems as if I have had to learn this lesson the hard way.

Such a lesson came after one of those long weekends. By long, I mean seventy-two hours straight of continuous search and rescue by two boat crews. By midday on Sunday, things had finally slowed down almost to a stop, and our relief was due to show up in just a few hours. We collapsed in the watch room, waiting for that time to pass.

While we were there, a staff car drove up to the base command post, and what appeared (by the markings on his hat) to be a captain and his aide proceeded through our location and on to the main operation center.

None of us moved or acknowledged them. It was not uncommon for Coast Guard reserve groups to come onto the base at different times during the weekend. For the most part, they were there to practice and prepare for when they would be called up to active duty. Sometimes the active members interfaced with the reserves; there were also times when each did their own thing.

If interaction was the theme of the day, there was usually a memo from the group office to coordinate the joint activity. When there was no such message, each group would proceed with their normal routine. In this way we would not interfere with each other's training or in the execution of our individual, day-to-day tasks. On this occasion no memo had been received; and because not a single crewmember had slept in seventy-two hours, exhaustion lulled us into complacency.

Let me make this very clear: whether an officer is reserve or active, they should command the same level of respect. A captain (who would be a full bird colonel in another service) is also easily distinguished by the gold markings on his hat that we call "scrambled eggs." There was absolutely no excuse for me or anyone else in the two crews to not give the recognition that these men deserved.

> The look on his face and his gesture immediately snapped me to attention.

Shortly after the two officers disappeared into the command room, the door cracked open a bit. The commander, who would have been the captain's aide, looked in my direction. As I was the only one in the room dressed in khaki, he pointed his finger and beckoned me forward. The look on his face and his gesture immediately snapped me to attention. As I came forward, I realized that I was once again in trouble.

Once I was in the command center, I stood at attention with my hat in my hand, looking straight ahead.

Captain B. turned to face me, and after a few minutes of reading me the riot act, finally calmed down and asked me what kind of station had so little respect for authority. And what kind of crews were working at this station? He then proceeded to tell me that he was not some weekend warrior, but a full captain in the United States Coast Guard. He deserved more respect than he had just received.

The commander then informed me that they were here to conduct an inspection of the lifeboat station, and that I had been informed of the inspection the previous week!

After a brief moment of silence, I spoke: "Sir, there is no excuse for my actions, sir! We did not know of your arrival, sir, but that again is no excuse for my actions today, sir."

Captain B.'s expression changed. He turned to his aide and asked when the itinerary had been sent. The commander said that it had been delivered and signed for on the previous Wednesday.

Captain B. turned back to me and asked what the current status was of the active crews resting in the next room.

Still standing at attention, I explained that both boats had been on continuous search and rescue for the last seventy-two hours, and they were waiting for their relief to arrive.

Now his expression was much more sympathetic. He asked me one more time: was I telling him that they had been up nonstop for seventy-two hours? To which I responded, "Yes sir!"

With a perplexed look, he asked if my commanding officer was on the base. I informed him that he lived in one of the houses by the lighthouse.

"Well, he should have been here to greet me, because I know the message was received by the station."

In my head I knew that the chief warrant officer of the station, CWO-4 Sam, did not like me. I also knew that he had probably been chuckling over what would happen when this captain arrived.

Captain B. turned to his aide and told him that he wanted to see the commanding officer as soon as possible.

It always feels strange when someone asks for something while you're standing in the room, all the while knowing that you're the one that's going to have to retrieve that item or person. Sometimes that's the military way. The commander turned to me and told me to get the CWO on the phone as soon as possible. Then he said, "For goodness' sake, relax."

Since the fastest way to communicate was from the command post we were in, I used the speakerphone that was in front of the duty watchmen.

When CWO-4 Sam answered, I said, "Chief Warrant Officer, there's a Captain B. here to see you. He has come to perform an inspection of the base."

Not knowing the speakerphone was on, he replied that he knew he was supposed to come, but he was too busy. I could handle it. Then he said, "Just tell him that I'm out of town," and hung up.

Captain B. went from cordial to irate in seconds. If there had been a smoke detector over his head, I'm sure it would have gone off!

I asked the captain if he wanted me to give him a tour of the station. He replied, "Absolutely! But not until I've had a chance to talk to your commanding officer! I want to start the tour at his house, so lead the way, chief."

Needless to say, two things happen over the next two hours. One of them was the chewing out of CWO-4 Sam. The second was my befriending a captain who not only approved of the status of the station but also told me that if there was ever anything that I needed, to call him personally.

It turned out that Captain B. was on the admiral's staff at the third district office. He was also the Equal Rights Officer. This was something that would come in handy at a later date. In the meantime, I learned a valuable lesson: to treat everybody with the respect that they deserved.

We all are children of God, from the lowest person in the world's order of things to the highest earthly position. Christ died for each one of us so that we could be called the children of God.

Given this reality, every person deserves respect, and we should treat them as we would treat a prince!

CHAPTER 7: CREW ABUSE

And not only *that*, but we also glory in tribulations, knowing that tribulation produces perseverance; and perseverance, character; and character, hope. (Rom. 5:3, 4)

In my commitment to serve the Lord, I realized it would not take long before I would run into trouble with the military.

Though it is possible to serve the Lord and your government, the higher you go in management, the more difficult it becomes. As a chief petty officer, there were many men that were under my command. This doesn't sound like it should be an issue, but the truth is that what you command your men to do you are, in fact, doing yourself.

The most obvious problem I had to address was the Sabbath. The Sabbath is that special day when we seek to connect with God and abstain from our normal, everyday life. At the same time, I knew that search and rescue must go on. Just like in a hospital, life does not stop for twenty-four hours while we seek to connect with God. After much prayer I decided to try something a little different.

One weekend I announced to the crew that from then on, from Friday sundown until Saturday sundown, our work would be restricted to search and rescue. Their response was naturally to be overjoyed: no scraping, chipping, painting, or general cleaning!

Be careful what you commit to God and man! Over the next few years, on my weekends, my watch saw over 900 search and rescues per year. It was nonstop, and it didn't take long for the crew to ask if we could go back to the old schedule. I would jokingly respond, "I don't think that will make the search and rescue go away, and that is our primary function."

Being in my early twenties, I was closer in age to most of the crew than I was to the commanding officer. It soon became apparent that the crew were seeking out my advice rather than his, not only for their problems but for difficult situations they were facing at the station. This did not help the situation between the commanding officer and me.

Chief Warrant Officer Sam already had a difficult time connecting with crew members. He had been in the service for over thirty years, and it seemed like he was tired and wanted this whole military life to be over. Some of the crew jokingly said that he was so old that when God said, "Let there be land," CWO-4 Sam put in for shore duty! I know it is not good for an officer to fraternize with the enlisted men, so the age separation was a natural barrier. Still, there should be a barrier of respect, not of contempt.

When CWO-4 Sam's executive officer (XO), a chief boatswain's mate, was transferred out, they did not send an immediate replacement. Already assigned to Station Eaton's Neck was a petty officer first-class boatswain's mate named Shore who had obviously been passed over many times for advancement.

CWO-4 Sam appointed BM1 Shore as his second-in-command. Instead of being upset, I was relieved. The boatswain's rating is designed to be a leadership rating; and though I was a chief petty officer, I was an electronics specialist. I had enough work without having to also fulfill the command duties of an XO.

My dear friend Chief Machinist Mate John did not want the position either, but he felt that the promotion of Shore was inappropriate. Among his concerns were the apparent dishonesty and cruelty of BM1 Shore; traits Shore shared with CWO-4 Sam.

Chapter 7: Crew Abuse

For example, some local fishing boats had been using the Coast Guard facilities to beat the others to market. From time to time, they also were seen refueling with Coast Guard fuel. And the lobsters and shellfish CWO-4 Sam and BM1 Shore were barbecuing had to come from somewhere ... but it wasn't the market.

So it really was no surprise when Chief John and I received a request from Coast Guard Intelligence (CGI) to come in for an interview. It also did not seem strange when they requested that this be done in secret.

Thinking that someone had tipped off CGI, we assumed the worst. However, all they asked about was whether we had seen any drugs or drug-related activity around the base. They had no interest in any of the other activities, so the interview did not last long.

We had always suspected that CWO-4 Sam had connections in high places. We also knew that things might be different back at the base. As we feared, CWO-4 Sam became more and more hostile, not just to Chief John and me but to the crew as well.

Life on a lifeboat station is not only very busy but can also be very dangerous. One day a boat crew leader had an accident and broke his leg. Normally in a situation like this, that crew member would be given time to recuperate. Quite often he would be given the chance to take leave, either out of his own pool or using an extended leave called sick leave. This would have allowed his leg to heal and would have eliminated more problems.

However, this young man was not given that opportunity. Instead he was told to stand watches on desk duty on a continuous basis. The cramped quarters of the command post made that difficult to do with his leg in a cast. After several weeks he had to have his leg rebroken by the doctors.

One of this young man's shipmates (and closest friend) took severe exception to this situation. Going to the commanding officer, he boldly threatened to write to his congressman.

CWO-4 Sam merely looked at him and laughed. "You are welcome to do whatever you think you can do," he answered, "but you better tread lightly."

The young man had left out one important detail: Senator Strom Thurmond, Chairman of the Armed Forces Committee, was his uncle.

I'd say that was a pretty important detail! Senator Thurmond initiated a congressional investigation.

When you commit yourself to Jesus, do not expect everything to be a bed of roses! In the book of John, Jesus tells his disciples, "If the world hates you, you know that it hated Me before *it hated* you. If you were of the world, the world would love its own. Yet because you are not of the world, but I chose you out of the world, therefore the world hates you" (John 15:18, 19).

If you think that baptism is going to change anything in your life that hasn't already changed, you are greatly mistaken. I often tell my baptismal candidates that baptism just makes you wet; the change has to occur in your heart before you go into the water.

CHAPTER 8: FALSE CHARGES

And we know that all things work together for good to those who love God, to those who are the called according to *His* purpose. (Rom. 8:28)

The normal procedure in a congressional investigation is for the Coast Guard to assign an investigating officer who will review the facts, interview the crew, and submit his report. The intent in the case of the young man with the broken leg was to choose a totally impartial officer, but instead the investigating officer, Lieutenant Cupp, was someone closely tied to both the CWO and the command at Group Long Island Sound (I would think it would be hard to be impartial under these conditions).

When Lieutenant Cupp arrived at the station, he came to me and asked where I wanted him to set up. I thought this a bit strange because I was not the commanding officer or even the executive officer, so I referred him to them.

Each of us from the lowest seaman to the commanding officer was interviewed and our statements recorded. After several days the process was complete, and Lieutenant Cupp returned to the group command. Chief John and I thought that perhaps now something would be done about the behavior of our commanding officers. My father had always taught me that the most powerful tool you possessed was the truth. Unfortunately, I also naïvely believed that the truth would always win in this world.

This is not a world of truth; this is a world of sin. As hard as it is to understand, sin is not always resolved with justice. God tells us, "I have stretched out My hands all day long to a rebellious people, who walk in a way *that* is not good, according to their own thoughts; a people who provoked Me to anger continually to my face" (Isaiah 65:2, 3a).

> When the report declaring the charges arrived two weeks later, my world came crashing down.

When the report declaring the charges arrived two weeks later, my world came crashing down. The investigation declared that Chief John and I were the source of the problem. It further stated that we had remonstrated against command (more commonly referred to as mutiny) and that I was enforcing religious beliefs on the crew.

We each received an Article 15, the military's version of a one man judge and jury. The date for our tribunal was set for one week from that day. We were to face the group commander in a captain's mast (a form of non-judicial punishment).

Not sure what to do or who to turn to, I called Pastor Nick and asked for his advice. Though he was as shocked as I was, he was able to calmly look at the situation and offer suggestions.

Meanwhile, knowing the connection between CWO Sam and the group commander, I thought my best course of action would be to

Chapter 8: False Charges

refuse the captain's mast and request a full court-martial. This is an option which enlisted men have that gives them a trial by jury instead of a single judge. I could also request that the jury consist of at least four enlisted men.

The real problem was that I did not have legal representation. I would also need that to prepare my case. I called and requested someone from the judge advocate general service (JAG, or military lawyers) and was told that I would get my lawyer the day of the trial. Somehow things seemed to be stacking against me.

Pastor Nick noticed the religious basis of the charges and suggested that I might be able to enlist church lawyers from the Adventist General Conference. He was successful in doing this very thing, so I began to feel a little more at ease. Still, I was perplexed as to where these charges could have come from. I also didn't know how the investigative report actually described events.

When we finally received that discovery report, it became clear that every person's testimony was slanted against Chief John and me. *How could this be?* I thought. Why would the crew have reported so many items incorrectly and been so unfavorable to both of us? Immediately I turned to the testimony of one of my closest friends, another electronic specialist that worked under me. His testimony was very damaging.

It just did not seem like the fellow I knew. Taking the report to him, I asked why he had said so many things which were obviously untrue.

Perplexed, he took the report and read his own testimony. When he had finished, he looked at me and stated that he had never said any of those things.

Now I began to see what was happening. Going from man to man, I had each of them read their testimony, only to find that their testimonies had also been altered to make me look like the person who needed to be set straight. One by one, I had them write affidavit statements declaring that, in fact, their testimonies had been changed to implicate me.

With this new ammunition in hand, I called Lieutenant Cupp. "Sir, I feel we have a major problem."

His response was that I was the one with the problem, not him … and that it would be taken care of soon enough.

When he had finished talking, I explained, "No, the problem is that I have affidavits from all of the men stating that their testimonies were altered!"

After a short period of silence, he hung up. The very next day, the charges were dropped.

I did not have time to rejoice, as a second set of charges soon replaced the first. This time I was alone in the charges, and I was now also accused of releasing the information in the report to the Long Island newspapers.

The only thing worse than creating problems within the Coast Guard is to take dirty laundry and expose it to the press. The story had, in fact, somehow made it out. But Pastor Nick was able to obtain a letter from the Long Island press stating that I was not the source of their story.

This, in and of itself, was a major step. I once again called Lieutenant Cupp, and in as non-threatening a way as possible, I told him that I *would* release the affidavits to the press if the charges were not again dismissed.

Once again the charges were dropped, but now I was given a letter of reprimand which would be put in my file. It said that I could not effectively represent the Coast Guard or its mission.

Since I was an enlisted man, such a letter was very unusual. Officers received letters of reprimand without the judicial process, but enlisted men did not. The normal procedure would have been to take me to a captain's mast or a court-martial. I brought this to the attention of the group command, but I was told that the letter would stand.

The only option available to me was to take the evidence that I had and bring it before a federal judge. Since the group command was in the third Coast Guard district, the nearest one was in New York City.

I obtained an audience with the federal judge, brought all of my documentation, laid out my case, and then waited for him to review the information. After his review, the ruling was sent to the group commander in East Haven, Connecticut. It required that the letter be removed from my file. If the group command wanted to pursue a form of punishment, it would have to be done through the court system.

Chapter 8: False Charges

My wife and I were relieved—actually, overjoyed—thinking we had finally won. Perhaps this was all behind us, and life would return to some form of normalcy.

That could not have been further from the truth.

After about one month, I received a call from a yeoman at Group Long Island Sound. Yeomen are the record keepers for the Coast Guard. They maintain personnel files and all written records relating to station operations. This particular yeoman was responsible for the personnel records of the men at the lifeboat station. He let me know that the letter still was in my file.

It had never been removed. All the prior evidence had already pointed to some form of conspiracy; this just amplified that situation. All of that anxiety, all of the fear, all of the questions flooded back into my mind. What was I going to do now?

I made an appointment to see the federal judge in New York one more time. I relayed the conversation that I had had with the yeoman and looked to him for advice.

It's amazing how quickly you can raise the ire of a federal judge by telling him his orders have been ignored. He looked at me, grabbed his coat, and said, "Let's go for a ride."

We drove to the group command in New Haven, Connecticut, where he asked to see the group commander. That person was actually a full commander in rank; the equivalent of a lieutenant colonel, which is a fairly powerful position. The judge then asked him if he could see my personnel file. The group commander responded by sending somebody to get it.

"No!" the judge said. "You do not understand. I want to pull it out of the file cabinet myself!" It was apparent that the judge did not trust the situation.

When we arrived at the file room, the judge opened the drawer, removed my file, and spread it out across the top of the cabinet. There, on the very top of the file, was the letter he had demanded be removed.

When a judge starts screaming at a commander, it is time to fade into the woodwork. I stepped back and watched the fireworks fly.

The net result came a few days later: a reprimand for the group commander, a reassignment for Lieutenant Cupp, and two chief warrant officers who would receive early retirement.

Several years later in Alaska, my sister met Lieutenant Cupp. He complained about a chief that had caused him to be buried there. She smiled and told him that he was talking about her brother, Chief Nickerson!

This is not the end of the story. It's only the beginning. There are many other involved parties that need to be introduced in their own stories. So we will put this one on hold while we introduce those players in their own right.

It is important to never lose sight of the leading hand of God! All our steps are in His control, and in the end, He will be glorified. Of course it does not feel that way while events transpire, but there can never be any question: God is always in control.

CHAPTER 9: WATER IN THE WAVEGUIDE

Be of the same mind toward one another. Do not set your mind on high things, but associate with the humble. Do not be wise in your own opinion. (Rom. 12:16)

The Bible clearly tells us to judge no one, yet we all at times think we're better than somebody else. The special meal for people who feel this way is called "humble pie." In this story I not only received humble pie but was given something to wash it down with.

Shortly after becoming chief, but before I was actually able to wear the new uniform, I was transferred to Group Long Island Sound. A brand-new electronics repair station was being established just off the sound in East Haven, Connecticut. The purpose of the station would be to augment all of the electronics personnel on stations and ships located within Long Island Sound. It would also be our job to calibrate and test all lighthouses and radio beacons up and down the coast from New London to New York City.

Having made chief at such a young age, I was a bit too sure of my abilities. My confidence was put to the test quickly enough when one of the small Coast Guard vessels, an eighty-two-foot patrol craft based out of New London, Connecticut, requested help in repairing their radar.

Many people may not be aware that a radar is an even simpler piece of equipment than a radio transmitter. There are a limited number of things that can go wrong. That is why, for the life of me, I could not understand why the three technicians who were assigned to New London (a petty officer first class, a petty officer second class, and a brand new petty officer third class) could not repair their own system.

Still, I was anxious to prove myself; to show the world that I had earned the rank that I had just received. I proceeded to that small vessel.

Now normally, when assisting in this manner, you would ask the technicians on the scene what they had done and exactly what they had checked. But anxious to prove my superior intelligence, I decided to skip this step and dig right into the system.

The two older technicians, who had been working on the system for over six hours, did not say anything. The young, new electronics technician (ET3), however, raised his hand.

I looked at him and said, "Not now! Let me take a look at the system first."

I put the device through its paces, checking each and every section and all of the voltages. I found absolutely nothing wrong, with one minor exception: the radar did not work. I stood back, looked at my notes, and proceeded to recheck each of the same points.

The definition of insanity is repeating the same steps over and over and expecting a different result. Here I was, redoing the same tests that I had just completed, but somehow expecting that there would be a different outcome. In case you haven't already guessed, the radar system still did not work.

Chapter 9: Water in the Waveguide

Once again the youngest guy present raised his hand. Knowing that this fellow couldn't be more than two weeks out of school, I figured that there was nothing he could add to what his superiors had already attempted. To prove that point, I looked at him and said, "All right, what do you have to say?"

He looked at me a bit sheepishly and said that maybe there was water in the waveguide.

Water in the waveguide! What a ridiculous idea. Didn't this fellow know anything about electronics?

Ignoring him, I went through all of the test points for the third time to make sure that I had not missed a single thing. Surprise, surprise! The radar still did not work ... and there was the young fellow, once more putting up his hand and asking if it was possible that there was water in the wave.

I explained to him that there were special clear shields placed at the top of the radar, and that around the outside of the antenna there was a sealed dome, together making it nearly impossible for water to get into the waveguide. As I spoke, I reached up above the radar set and pointed out the waveguide, then began to explain its principles to the ET3: that it was a hollow tube that allowed radar signals to bounce back and forth on their way to the antenna, from which the signals were then projected.

During my illustration, I put my hand on the waveguide. To my surprise, it was warm. This should not have been the case. The only way it could be warm was if something was absorbing the energy!

I disconnected the junction of the waveguide. I knew that there was a protection window between the unit itself and the wave. I was not sure what I was going to find. Moving it to one side, I leaned in to look inside.

As I slid the waveguide off of the transmitting unit, at least half a gallon of seawater poured down onto my face.

Some example of superior intelligence! I reconnected the waveguide, turned the system on, and we discovered that it was working beautifully.

Some of you have seen those commercials for Visa cards. Radar transmitting unit: $50,000. Two sections of waveguide: $50. The look on that young third class petty officer's face? Priceless!

One of the lessons I learned that day is that we need to be open to the opinions and help of everyone. There are no minor players in this world. Each and every person has a part to play and has valuable input. You need to remember to treat all men and women equally.

CHAPTER 10: FIRST REAL DUTY

Do all things without complaining and disputing, that you may become blameless and harmless, children of God without fault in the midst of a crooked and perverse generation, among whom you shine as lights in the world. (Phil. 2:14, 15)

Nobody likes the bad jobs, and nobody likes to do the mindless but necessary tasks, but these jobs are often for our own good.

We had just finished my first patrol aboard the Coast Guard cutter Active, and we were preparing to re-enter Portsmouth Harbor and tie up at the station. I was informed that it would be my duty to run the microphone cable to the quarterdeck shack as soon as the ship was tied up.

It might be helpful to point out that when I was first assigned to the ship, they were expecting a seaman electronics technician with a specialization in cryptographic and communications equipment; aka an SNETN, or the equivalent of a private. But they got me instead: an ETN3, which is one rank up, or in other words, a sergeant. How that happened is a story I won't tell in this book; let us just say that they were not ready to fit me into the schedule.

Unprepared to assign me duties befitting my rank, they had decided to put me on bridge watches and break me in with the radar men. This meant that during the two-week patrol, I was on watch from 4:00 to 8:00 a.m., worked a full day, then returned to do another watch at 4:00 p.m.

I'm sure it was not meant to be a pleasant situation, but I looked forward to it: whatever the radar men did during those hours, I wished to learn. In fact, they were able to instruct me in how to use a sextant, perform celestial navigation, and detect objects on the radar.

The commanding officer, Captain S., came to the bridge each morning at about 5 a.m. He would sit in his special captain's chair, which was elevated above and behind all the activity, to watch the sunrise and observe the crew. In the evening he returned. During those two weeks, he asked me numerous questions and learned pretty much all about my life.

Despite his rank and position, he was a friend to every man on that ship. He had come up through the ranks, literally: he had been an enlisted man and after one tour went on to Officer Candidate School. Because he excelled, they sent him on again to the Coast Guard Academy. This ship was his third command. There was no question in anyone's mind that he was going to go all the way to the top.

Returning to the story, the patrol was over. During that time, we had been through the eye of a Category 5 hurricane with winds in excess of 170 mph. By now I was anxious to get my feet once again on dry land! However, I had been told that I could not go on liberty until my last task was accomplished.

Wishing to do my best, I decided to run the cable while the ship was entering Portsmouth harbor. I also decided to make it the best cable run that there had ever been: hidden from view and running behind objects in such a way that it could be coiled up and ready to go. As soon as we tied to the pier, I would be able to plug it in and be on my way.

Chapter 10: First Real Duty

In the process of running the cable from the bridge, over the side, and down to the first level, I saw that there was a door between where I was and where I needed to go. I did not want to run the cable in front of the door. I really thought I should run it behind the door (up and over the top) so that no one would trip or get caught up in the cable.

On the door there was a sign that read, *Do not close this door*. Now, I could read: I knew they wanted the door left open. However, my job required running the cable *behind* the door.

I had no intentions of closing that door. I was only going to loosen the dogs (clamps) holding it against the side of the ship, run the cable behind it, and reconnect the dogs. What I didn't know was that behind those dogs there was a trip switch. As soon as I loosened them and pulled the door away from the bulkhead, the turbine engines shut down.

> On the door there was a sign that read, Do not close this door.

That cute little door with the *Do not close* sign was the air intake for the turbines which lived in the same space as the twin locomotive diesels. The two turbines were the same type of engines that are used on airplanes. They were not generally run at the same time as the diesels, but when they were ... well, it was absolutely amazing how much power that little cutter had at her disposal (I believe it could've pulled an aircraft carrier off dry ground!).

In short, the turbines required a large amount of air flowing through them, and that trip switch was there to prevent those engines from self-destructing. My action had tripped the switch. Because the diesel engines were off at the time, this left our vessel without power.

But no big deal, right? Just close the door quickly and everything will be all right. Not right! Because when I did that, the engines did not restart. It quickly became apparent that restarting those engines was not as simple as turning a key on a car.

I suppose that I need to explain that the current in Portsmouth Harbor can be so strong that it can pull the buoys underwater. A 210-foot cutter without engines is also at the mercies of that current. So our ship commenced to swinging in 360-degree circles in the middle of a busy harbor.

I saw frantic activity everywhere as the crew tried to get the engines restarted. In all of this excitement and confusion, the engineering chief warrant officer looked over the side of the ship and saw me standing there in front of the door with the cable still in my hand. "*YOU!*" he shouted, along with numerous other words I choose not to repeat. "Drop that cable and get up here *NOW!*"

Before the cable hit the ground, I was already two steps up the nearest ladder. The CWO yelled for a good fifteen minutes. I think—but I'm not sure—that all but about two minutes of that rant were not repeatable!

I was then hauled in before the captain. As visions of my newly-earned stripes disappearing ran through my brain, Captain S. just stood there while the CWO explained what had happened.

Captain S. raised his hand, smiled at me, and said, "Petty Officer Nickerson, have you learned anything from this experience?"

His tone of voice and actions put me at ease. I almost thought that I was going to get away with it. Captain S. told me that he did not want me to start my career with a black mark. What we were going to do instead would be off the record. I had no problem with this.

The captain turned to the engineering CWO and asked if there was a particular compartment that needed tender care. The CWO now began to smile as well. He asked if I had a toothbrush.

Totally confused, I said, "Yes sir!"

"Good," he continued, "Get your toothbrush and meet me on the flight deck."

I spent the next sixteen hours cleaning the aft hawser locker (the compartment at the end of the flight deck used to store all of the towing and docking hawsers). Of course, this was not before waving to my wife on the pier and informing her I might be a little late.

God has given us many *Do not close this door* signs in the Bible. Our biggest problem is that we just do not read them.

Probably the greatest collection of these instructions is found in Exodus chapter 20. We typically like to call them the Ten Commandments. These commandments are there for us to understand the character of God. However, instead of reading with that understanding, we want to condemn them as excessive requirements. And all too often we are not even sure what all of them say.

So take the time right now. Turn to Exodus 20 and scan through those commandments. Instead of looking at them as rules, think of them as keys to a relationship with the Creator of the universe. When we look at the Bible as a way for God to reach out and connect with us in a relationship, it can change everything we read.

CHAPTER 11: BOOT CAMP

Being confident of this very thing, that He who has begun a good work in you will complete *it* until the day of Jesus Christ.... (Phil. 1:6)

I suppose if there's any verse in the Bible that I consider my favorite, Philippians 1:6 meets the criteria. I guess I must consider myself a work in progress. On a related note, many have asked me, how did I ever end up in the Coast Guard? That in itself is an interesting story.

The year was 1968, and I was just beginning another semester as an art and math student at Atlantic Union College. I am not proud of the fact that I was abusing my body to fulfill my school dreams. I literally worked 120 hours a week during the summer and 60 hours a week during the school year, which left little time for sleep (it is important to remember that your body is a temple of God. It is not always others that cause our problems; many times we abuse the gifts that God has given us).

Chapter 11: Boot Camp

So it was that in January of that year, I collapsed and was taken to the hospital. Then, three days after dropping out of school, I received my draft notice to report to the US Army in mid-June.

Young people today do not have an active draft. Even though they are required to sign up, they do not realize what was happening during the Vietnam War. This time of my life was during the Tet Offensive: if you were not in school you were being taken into the service.

When I had registered on my eighteenth birthday, I had received a 1-A-0 classification. This meant that I was eligible for noncombatant duty only. In the nearly two years since then, many of my noncombatant friends had died.

Because I was in the hospital, the Army agreed to give me several months to recuperate. Because the life expectancy for corpsman was very short, I considered alternatives. However, none of the available options appealed to me. I reconciled myself to going into the Army.

After getting out of the hospital and while waiting for my June induction date, I worked at Digital Equipment Corporation in Maynard, Massachusetts, near where I lived in Lancaster. One weekend after visiting my parents in Fairhaven, I was heading back home. Shortly after crossing the New Bedford Bridge, I heard a radio announcement that there were two openings in the US Coast Guard. The customs house just happened to be two blocks from where I was driving right then, and it only took me a few seconds to realize this might be a better opportunity than the Army.

Lorelei, at the time my *future* wife, had a brother in the Coast Guard. We had previously talked about my joining as well, but it had appeared impossible. Now, though, I was the first one to respond to that ad, only minutes after it broadcast. The recruiter told me that the induction date for the Coast Guard was July 1, 1968.

Now I had two new concerns that needed to be addressed. One, I needed to be in the Coast Guard before my June Army induction date. Two, I also needed to change my classification from 1-A-0 to 1-A in order to join the Coast Guard.

I assumed that the classification change would be no problem, as I probably would not see combat service in the Coast Guard. The first item, however, posed a greater difficulty. With the draft, if you received your notice, you could only join another service if you could actually be *in* it before your original induction date.

When I told the recruiter this, he looked at me and said, "That is not a problem." He told me to raise my hand, and he swore me in right there. Then he told me that I was going to use my first thirty days of leave before going to boot camp!

I met the bus at the customs house on July 1, 1968, and rode down to Cape May, New Jersey. I was excited about what was going to happen. I had no idea what to expect in boot camp, but I knew that my brother had just completed his with the Army. How bad could it be in the Coast Guard?

I soon learned that not only do they push you to the physical limits, they push the mental as well. I was assigned to Kilo Company, and our drill instructor was a former Navy SEAL! There was nothing that he asked us to do that he couldn't do twice over!

The whole purpose of boot camp is to enforce conformity; to make everybody respond without question and to their maximum limits. I found that if you did everything they said and pushed yourself as hard as you possibly could, they could tell. Some endured a lot of abuse, but those who followed that basic principle ("Do it till you drop") fared much better.

Boot camp usually lasted eight weeks, but after just under six weeks, the young fellow assigned to doing the illustrations and drawings for the training aids was transferred. Those in charge knew that I had been an art major in college, and they asked if I would be interested in getting out of boot camp two weeks early to spend some time drawing their training aids instead.

They did not have to ask me twice! No more hours of marching with my sea bag over my head or long periods of calisthenics, and no more 4 a.m. runs! I stayed and did that work for a few extra weeks, but then a regular replacement arrived to take over my artistic duties. All good things must come to an end.

The next step would be either a direct transfer to a ship or to some type of Class A school. I had put in requests for corpsman and cook school. I was just a little surprised when I received orders for electronics school. When I asked why, they just told me that because I was also a mathematics major in college, they felt that this would be the best selection.

It is interesting to note that of my company in boot camp (a total of thirty men), ten of those men had graduate degrees, eighteen others had undergraduate degrees, and only two of us had not finished our undergraduate programs. One of the fellows in my company had a master's in marine biology, and they made him a cook! My brother in the Army had an associate degree in electronics, and they made him a truck driver! It became apparent that there was no rhyme or reason to the selection process, but I figured that I could do worse than electronics.

Some may question why this story is in this book at all. I include it because there are some who say that because of the things I've done and the places that I've been, I am just another driven person. I would contend that there is a difference between driven and directed.

I began with the text from Philippians chapter 1, verse 6. This Bible passage tells us that when Jesus begins a good work in us, He'll fulfill it until He returns.

Whatever I have done and wherever I have gone, it has all been the result of direction, not of one who is self-driven. This is an important distinction, for when we realize that by ourselves we can do nothing, we can begin to understand that the direction our lives take is set by a greater power.

There are no coincidences in this life. In fact, the concept does not even exist except in our minds. It was no coincidence that I happened to be near the New Bedford customs house. It was no coincidence that the recruiter was able to override my draft. And it was no coincidence that the government decided I would be better suited in electronics than as a cook or a corpsman.

Stop and look at your life. Under careful examination, each of us can see how we have been directed. We can fight that direction, and we can seek our own way, but when we do, we will fail.

CHAPTER 12:
EYE OF THE STORM

For He shall give His angels charge over you, to keep you in all your ways. (Ps. 91:11)

The twenty-four weeks of electronics school went by fairly fast. I quickly found that my mathematics background helped tremendously in understanding basic electronics. I also soon began to realize how much I enjoyed the subject. Even at this early stage, I considered continuing in the field when my tour of duty was done.

I came out at the top of my class, and the Coast Guard offered me four more months of schooling. They initially just told me that it was communications school, but in fact it was cryptography school (it was also run by the US Navy rather than the Coast Guard). This school consisted of two separate seven-and-a-half week programs. Each one covered a different piece of communications equipment essential to every ship.

Chapter 12: Eye of the Storm

I discovered a method of troubleshooting that allowed me to find the problems in equipment during the testing phase faster than anybody else. In part because of this, I received perfect scores in the first school. I continued to do so in the second school up until the final exam.

Each quiz or test consisted of equipment with a series of possible malfunctions. The instructor would place some defective components in your piece of equipment, and you had to repair it within fifteen minutes. For every additional five minutes you took, your score was reduced.

Up until that final exam, there had always only been one defect in each piece of equipment. However, on the final exam, the instructor put six defects in my piece of equipment. Every time I found a problem he would look at me, smile, and say, "There's one more."

I finally found the last one after a total of twenty-five minutes. This accounted for a drop in my overall average of two hundredths of a point. Because of this prank by the teacher and the other students, I ended up with a 99.98 average for the two programs combined.

The final piece of equipment that I had worked on needed to receive a sync signal every five minutes. If you missed the sync signal, you would have to wait five minutes for the next one. Or so most people thought, as they stood around and waited the whole five minutes before proceeding. However, to waste five minutes is to let precious time slide by. Time can be crucial if you're waiting for an important encoded signal, and there are many ways to check a piece of equipment without having the sync signal.

There are many people, young and old, who believe they have to get in sync with God before they can accept Him. But the amazing thing about Jesus is that He takes you where you are and begins to change your life. You don't need to change your life *before* He can take you. Precious time is lost, and precious souls are probably lost, because they're waiting for the sync signal. Jesus can troubleshoot your life without the wait.

Because of my standing in the class, I was offered a shore station in San Juan, Puerto Rico. This was, in fact, a Navy station, and I would have been transferred to the US Navy (each Coast Guard ship utilized crypto equipment, but the transmitting sites were Navy-manned; I was unaware of this during the following sequence of events). In addition to the shore station offer, I was promoted to the rank of Petty Officer Third Class. I found out later that the Coast Guard was not pleased with this promotion, but they had to accept it since I was under the command of the Navy at the time.

When I completed cryptography school, Lorelei was pregnant with our first child. She was apprehensive, and rightly so, about going to San Juan and giving birth so far from family. This assignment would, in fact, probably mean that it would be several years before we could reconnect with family. So since the Coast Guard had offered me any station that had my particular rating, I asked Lorelei where she would like to go. We agreed on Portsmouth, New Hampshire.

In Portsmouth there were two Coast Guard ships: the Active and the Decisive. Both were 210-foot, medium-endurance cutters. I don't know who chose the names for this class of vessel, but all of them were so fitting. Why did I ask for the Active instead of the Decisive? I will never know, except to understand that there are no coincidences.

When I contacted the Coast Guard placement office and told them that I desired to go to the Active, they paused and asked me if I was *sure* that I wanted this over San Juan, Puerto Rico (to this day I have never been to Puerto Rico; I have, however, been to the Dominican Republic … I can only envision how "difficult" the duty might have been on those beaches!).

When I reported to my new cutter and explained that I had volunteered for this post, the yeoman receiving my orders looked at me as if I had six heads. His only comment was, "You volunteered for this duty?"

Immediately alarms went off. I said, "Why do you ask that?"

He asked me if I knew what this cutter's mission entailed.

I answered, "Of course: search and rescue!"

He smiled and informed me that, yes, they did do search and rescue; but in addition, they found the eye of hurricanes, in order to go into storms and log information found only on the surface inside the eye.

My first thought was, *how bad can it be?* The answer came when we got underway two days later, in the month of August in 1969.

Chapter 12: Eye of the Storm

I had been assigned the 4:00 to 8:00 radar watch. I was standing watch alone when the duty officer, Master Chief Boatswain's Mate Jenkins, came and told me to look for an island on the radar.

I informed him that there were no islands near where we were located (at the time we were at least 300 miles from the nearest land). With a smirk on his face, he told me to do as I was told.

It hadn't taken me long to figure out how to distinguish objects on a radar. It was easy to identify land and ships (by the way, I often wonder how people that made navigation charts back then could depict the shoreline so accurately. I know how they are able to do it *now*, but even the old charts are fairly accurate). Within a few hours, I saw what appeared to be an island ... where there was no island.

It seemed to be a significant body of land at least twelve miles across. That's the size of Nantucket! The radar was capable of seeing fifty miles in each direction, so that twelve-mile island took up quite a large section of one quadrant.

I let the master chief know what I had detected. He immediately asked for the bearing. Taking a bearing on the center of the island, I relayed the information to him. The master chief turned to the helmsman and told him, "Make it so."

Yes, we really talked like that! This was the command to make a course for the bearing I had just given. My first thought was, *this should be interesting*, because we were bearing down on that island fairly fast. And the island was coming towards us just as fast as we were going toward it; a situation that just did not make sense.

Master Chief Jenkins then told me to let him know the minute we were in the sea chatter. Sea chatter was the pickup of the waves near the shore of an island, and it tended to obscure the actual coastline. It also designated where the water was shallow and thus dangerous to a ship. As we came within fifty yards of the "island," I informed the master chief.

You may be interested to learn that 1969 saw the greatest number of hurricane-status storms on the East Coast (twelve) in the twentieth century. That day in August, we headed into the eye of Hurricane Camille; a Class 5 hurricane with winds in excess of 170 mph! How do I know today what the wind speed was? I was about to record it! But first, I was about to find out just how hard it really was to get into the eye of a hurricane.

It is worth noting that visibility was less than twenty feet. This meant that from the bridge, we could barely see the bow. The master chief announced on the PA system to prepare for the eye. As soon as he had done so, he went to the engine annunciators.

It's hard to describe what entering the eye of a Class 5 hurricane entails. Yes, we were a 210-foot cutter, but that is *small* in 100-foot waves, 175 mph winds, and rain that is going sideways as much and as hard as it's coming down.

The annunciators were the controls that relayed information directly to the engine room for the adjustment of the propellers' pitch. The engines' shafts were always running at full, and the speed was adjusted primarily by changing the pitch of the propellers. There were two, and by adjusting the pitch of one over the other, the ship could do a controlled 360-degree turn in less than its own length. For the master chief to steer the ship this way allowed for far greater maneuverability than just using the rudder.

> I was about to find out just how hard it really was to get into the eye of a hurricane.

What appeared on the radar to be the ship striking the island was, in actuality, the ship entering the eye of the storm. The wind at this point was at its maximum. To prevent the ship from being spun like a top, the master chief put one of the propellers in full reverse and the other to full forward. This action counteracted the wind as we broke into the eye.

It is also hard to describe what the inside of the eye of a hurricane looks like. The best I can do is to say that you are in a sort of can which consists of a wall of water all around the eye that seems to go all the way up to the sky. The waves are still ferocious, but there is no wind whatsoever. You can even see clear, beautiful, blue sky above you!

As the storm passed over us and we approached the far side of the eye, I asked the master chief if there would be a way to travel in the eye for a while. He informed me that we would not be able to keep up with the storm and that it would not be a good situation to have the storm overtake us from behind. He went on to say, "But that's not the bad news. The bad news is, the backside of a hurricane is worse than the front."

As we approached the edge of the can that we were in, I watched the bow disappear into the solid wall of water that constituted the edge of the eye. The master chief repeated the procedure he had done upon entering the eye in order to prevent the ship from being spun like a top.

During my time aboard the Active, the cutter entered over twenty hurricanes and numerous tropical storms. In our lives we face many hurricanes, and there are times when it feels like we are just riding in a lull between storms.

But it's important to understand that God is with us no matter what storm arrives. Jesus tells us that He will never leave us nor forsake us. There will be times when we feel like we're facing certain death, but these are also the times when He is most greatly with us.

We cannot always distinguish, with the radar of life, the difference between what seems like sheer death and what is only the eye of a storm. Jesus has been there and done that. He has been tempted in all the ways we have. Always trust in the Lord, and you can weather any storm.

CHAPTER 13: NO LIFEBOAT?

Give ear, O Lord, to my prayer; and attend to the voice of my supplications. In the day of my trouble I will call upon You, for You will answer me. (Ps. 86:6, 7)

Have you ever felt alone? I mean *totally* alone? Have you ever been in a situation where you realized that there was no one who could help you?

Hurricanes aside, I was the Active's new cryptographic specialist. So in those first days, I received a tour of the ship and was then shown to the crypto room, where I was given an explanation of my duties.

The crypto room was off of the radio room and no bigger than about 6' x 6'. In this room were located two types of crypto equipment, all of the codes, and classified plans for the ship.

One of my responsibilities was to sync and enter the daily codes. These consisted of what looked like tickets marked with numerous

Chapter 13: No Lifeboat?

holes, which I inserted into one machine with a key punch slot that had been supplied by Coast Guard command. The ship carried a supply of those codes that would last thirty days (one for each day). Each card was shredded by the machine after insertion. That shredded material was then placed in a blender and mixed with water to form a pasty ball.

The other machine received a sync signal from the command center. This sync signal was sent every five minutes and was randomly generated from noise (like that sound you hear on a radio frequency where there is no station). After the sync signal was received, each piece of equipment would then generate its own code. This made communication between the shore and our ship unique.

> While I slept, there was a severe emergency: a fire in the engine room.

I found all of this interesting until I was informed of the ramifications of my position: though the equipment was operated by the radio men, I was responsible not only for the security of the crypto gear but also, in case of emergency, for the destruction of the equipment, the spare parts, and the codes. Furthermore (I was informed), because of these duties, I did not have a lifeboat billet.

A billet was a spot on one of the lifeboats. Without one, you would either go down with the ship or, after destroying the equipment, jump over the side and make your way to the nearest lifeboat.

They did offer me an inflatable life vest, which I kept in the crypto room, but this was cheap comfort considering my responsibilities. Many will remember the US Navy vessel Pueblo and the capture of its crew. In that episode only one life was lost: that of the crypto specialist. He was shot while in the process of destroying the codes.

On one particular evening, I had just been relieved from watch and settled into my bunk. As I have mentioned before, at that time in my life, I could sleep anywhere at any time. Besides, between eight hours of watch and eight hours of duty, I often went with little sleep.

While I slept, there was a severe emergency: a fire in the engine room.

There is perhaps no greater fear on a ship. The turbines are very effective at propelling the ship, but their special aviation fuel is very explosive. The fire progressed to the point where the captain felt it necessary for the crew to stand by in the lifeboats. The general alarm was sounded, and the lifeboats were lowered while the fire crew endeavored to put the fire out.

Once the fire was extinguished, the boats were reloaded, one by one, onto the ship. Each man was counted based on his lifeboat billet and position in the fire crew. When the count was complete, they realized there was one man missing. I was that missing man.

They began a search … but it did not take long to discover that I had slept through the entire emergency!

Without a lifeboat billet, the individual boats had not reported me missing. Apparently, this had not happened on the ship in the past (I can only hope that it was not the first time this had occurred *anywhere*).

The captain and I had developed a good bond, and he was concerned about the potential risks of this situation. He decided that although I did not have a lifeboat billet, in an emergency I was to report to the number one lifeboat before going back to perform my duties. It was also decided that in any general emergency, the duty officer would make sure that I was awake.

As embarrassing as these events may have been, it was a source of comfort to know that I was being watched over. Each of us can feel the same comfort by knowing that Jesus is watching over us. We can all have a lifeboat billet regardless of our occupation, gender, or age. It is called the bosom of Abraham, and it is available to all who believe in Jesus Christ.

When life is dark and dreary and there seems to be no chance of survival, reach out to Jesus. He hears your prayers. And though at times it may seem like there is nobody listening, He is always there. He can heal your broken heart, pull you from the deepest depression, and share your deepest sorrow.

What about when things are great? Jesus is there as well to offer friendship and security. Don't just wait for disaster to call on Jesus. Consider Him a friend you can talk to about anything! He is there to provide comfort and security regardless of the situation.

CHAPTER 14: THE KEO

My sheep hear My voice, and I know them, and they follow Me. (John 10:27)

After passing through a particularly nasty storm, we received an urgent message telling us to go back through it. I mentioned before that the backside of a hurricane is worse than the front, so it was not encouraging news when the announcement was made. Why were we going back? The Keo, a Liberian oil tanker, was trying to make port. However, they were in the path of the hurricane.

The tanker was larger than a football field and held millions of gallons of crude oil. To make matters worse, it had been discovered (or it had been leaked) that the owners had filled many of the voids in the hull with oil. Those voids were there for buoyancy, and misusing them could seriously affect the stability of the vessel.

The storm had stalled some 300 miles off the coast of Norfolk, Virginia. This gave us an opportunity: we hoped to reach the vessel before the eye of the storm did.

In the meantime the captain called the tanker on the radio and relayed the information that he had learned. He attempted to get them to change course before the hurricane overtook them. Unfortunately, the captain of the tanker did not believe him and decided to continue on his course. There appeared to be nothing our captain could say to convince him otherwise.

Sensing the disaster that appeared to be on the horizon, our captain suggested that their crew stay near the stern of their vessel. Normally on these vessels, if they broke apart, the bow would last longer than the stern; but given the illegal filling of the voids in the bow, that safety feature would no longer work.

As we fought our way back through the hurricane, we received a radio message that their ship was beginning to break up. Once again, our captain tried to encourage the crew to go to the stern, but they opted for the bow.

By the time we arrived, the bow had sunk like a rock. The stern was still afloat. All thirty-five crewmen of the tanker were lost.

It was strange to hear the radio broadcast stating that the Coast Guard was on scene and had the situation under control. In reality, we were fighting for our *own* lives in the debris of the tanker.

We searched for survivors but found only oil-covered bodies, some only half there in the shark-infested waters. I still can remember retrieving those bodies quite vividly.

Not only was this a tremendous natural disaster in terms of lives lost; it was also the largest oil spill off our coast until the spill of the Valdez. It is a bit ironic that, many years later, the first response vessel to the Valdez was the Active; but by then I had left the ship.

Thirty-five men were lost because one man decided to ignore the warnings. We can either heed God's warnings or ignore them. One course leads to salvation; the second course leads to ultimate destruction.

Jesus is always calling each and every one of us. The Bible tells us to "… work out your own salvation with fear and trembling; for it is God

Chapter 14: The Keo

who works in you both to will and to do for *His* good pleasure" (Phil. 2:12b, 13). This does not mean that our salvation is based on works but rather that we alone are responsible for our salvation.

These verses also clearly let us know that God will continue to work in our lives so that we can make the correct choices, but no one can make the decision for us. Only we bear that responsibility. This is probably the hardest lesson for a parent to understand: we cannot save our children (although this does not eliminate the need for every parent to give each child the tools to understand how to make their own decision about salvation).

God has no desire that any man be lost. He would have all mankind receive eternal life, but that is not going to happen. This world is soon coming to its close. The warnings that Jesus has given us are visible all around us. How can we improve our chances of hearing Him?

The Holy Spirit encourages each one of us to form that relationship with Jesus Christ. The only way to do so is to spend time with Christ, and the only way to truly do *that* is to spend time in His Word. Romans 10:17 reminds us that faith comes by hearing and hearing by the Word of God. There are many good books and many good authors, but there is no substitute for spending time in Scripture.

CHAPTER 15: SIMUS KUDIRKA

For I say, through the grace given to me, to everyone who is among you, not to think of *himself* more highly than he ought to think, but to think soberly, as God has dealt to each one a measure of faith. (Rom. 12:3)

Where do we get our faith? Do we get it by just trying harder? It is unfortunate that most people think that this is how faith is improved, when the only thing that we can do on our own is to focus on Jesus Christ. Paul tells us that faith comes by hearing and hearing by the Word of God (Rom. 10:17). There is no substitute for reading God's Word. When we do, it changes our lives.

Sometimes when I tell the following story, people then do research and tell me that some of the events I describe are not recorded. I realize this may be true. Some of these events are from my own experience, whether they were recorded or not.

Chapter 15: Simus Kudirka

Let's start at the beginning: our mission was to provide support while the diplomats were resolving some fishing issues with Russia. Because of the talks that were being conducted, one of their mother ships was anchored just five miles off the coast of Martha's Vineyard.

The Russian fishing fleet was a sight to behold. There were times when we would come up to the fleet at night, and it would look like we were approaching New York City. The mother ship was especially interesting: it was as big as a football field. When we were alongside her, we felt like we were a toy bobbing on the ocean. The top of our mast didn't even come up to the mother ship's first deck. However, there were numerous little patio-like windows on different decks below the main deck, and at times we would see Russian sailors on these levels.

We had been alongside them for over a week, and we were now relieved by our sister ship, the cutter Vigilant. The crew was anxious to return to port because of how long we had been away.

Just before we tied up in Newcastle, the captain addressed the crew to remind us of the importance of our mission. He also reminded us that we could be recalled at any time, and informed us that we were to travel no farther than two hours away from port.

My wife's parents lived in South Lancaster, Massachusetts; only about one-and-a-quarter hours away. It seemed very logical to me that if I was one-and-a-quarter hours away, I could get back to the ship within the two-hour window (the only possible fly in my ointment would be getting recalled as soon as I left the ship!). So Lorelei met me at the ship when we docked, and from Newcastle we headed straight for South Lancaster, Massachusetts.

We arrived about seventy-five minutes later, where my mother-in-law met us in the driveway. She told me there had been a phone call stating that I was to return to the ship. I asked her when the phone call had arrived, and she told me, "About one hour ago."

This was the worst case scenario! I knew that it would be near-impossible for me to reach the ship within the required time. Still, I was going to give it my best shot.

I assumed that if I were speeding, I would be stopped by the police, which would give me an excuse for being late. However, I soon realized that if you *want* a police officer, there is none to be found. I did arrive at the ship in approximately one hour … only fifteen minutes past the deadline.

When I got there, the engines were running and all lines but one had already been removed from the dock. The captain on the bridge told me to leave the car on the pier, leave the keys in it, and jump onboard.

It appeared they had been waiting for me to arrive, because I was directed immediately to the crypto room. They had been unable to communicate with the Vigilant and wanted me to check the equipment. It did not take me long to find out that our equipment was working just fine. There was a problem on the Vigilant's end.

The Vigilant had had to withdraw from the side of the Russian mother ship. In their haste, their long wire antenna (by means of which all cryptographic communications were transmitted) had been caught in the rigging of the mother ship and broken.

I do not know why the Vigilant's crypto technician had not shifted to one of their other antennas, but this situation now created two problems: First, the entire world would hear what was about to transpire. Second, we needed to arrive as soon as possible to restore confidentiality to the situation.

It took only about fifteen minutes to clear Portsmouth Harbor. From there we headed directly to Cape Cod Canal; a trip of several hours.

I have been through the canal many times, and it is usually a slow process. In this case, though, the captain had radioed ahead and had the Coast Guard station there prepare it for our arrival. All traffic was moved out of the canal as fast as possible, and new vessels were not allowed to enter. When we reached the canal we went through at a high rate of speed. I was glad there were no other vessels inside it.

We arrived at Martha's Vineyard some eight hours after our departure. Between monitoring the radio broadcasts, talking to some of the crewmembers of the Vigilant, and what I experienced firsthand, here is what transpired during that eight hour period.

The Vigilant had picked up the talks where we had left off. Meanwhile onboard the Russian mother ship was a young man named Simus Kudirka.

Chapter 15: Simus Kudirka

Simus was their radio operator and cryptologist (a position I can relate to). For many years he had dreamed of what freedom would be like, for Simus was a Christian in a non-Christian world. Worship and religion of any kind in his home country of Lithuania were not possible at that time in Earth's history.

Simus had heard many stories about the United States and how freedom of religion was a real opportunity. He had even had the chance to hear Radio Free America broadcasts, which gave him hope. And now he could see Martha's Vineyard less than five miles away!

I'm not sure if he was a strong enough swimmer to attempt to cross the distance to Martha's Vineyard, but difficult situations call for difficult choices. *Hope is a power ....* It is hard for us to understand what true persecution is or what those who experience it are willing to do in order to worship openly. Hope can drive men not only to perform amazing feats but to attempt what might be considered impossible.

Whether or not he considered swimming, it appears that the thought of defection had more than once occurred to Simus. When he had seen the Active leave, he had feared that he might not get another opportunity. But then the Vigilant had arrived, the talks continued, and he realized he had been given a second chance.

> *Simus saw his opportunity and seized the day. He jumped from the Russian mother ship onto the cutter's flight deck!*

How far would you go to be able to freely worship? How important is your connection with Jesus Christ? There are those who feel that this connection is the most important thing in this life. There is nothing the devil can do to stop their desire to be with Jesus.

One of the mini decks on the mother ship was located just a few feet above the flight deck of the Vigilant. Freedom was just those precious feet away. In Simus's mind that meant it was within his grasp.

While the Vigilant was tied to the Russian mother ship, the protocol was to keep the ship's engines active so that in an emergency the cutter could move away. There were also numerous guards on the cutter who were ready to detect any problem. However, there was one problem they had not anticipated.

Simus saw his opportunity and seized the day. He jumped from the Russian mother ship onto the cutter's flight deck! He survived the fall, but he twisted his ankle and needed the crew's assistance to stand.

Captain E. of the Vigilant happened to be on the bridge at the time of the incident. He recognized the seriousness of the situation, ordered the lines cut, and put the cutter underway, moving away from the Russian ship. The entire process only took a few minutes, and it was then that the long wire antenna, which ran from the mast to the stern, caught on the Russian ship's rigging and broke.

The cutter stopped about 100 yards away from the Russian ship while the captain tried to decide what to do next. He had no idea who the jumper was. His only concerns were for the safety of his ship and his crew. Meanwhile it did not take long for the Russians to realize not only what had happened but who the sailor was.

Throughout the history of defectors, far more attention has always been paid to those with the potential to impact secrets of governments or companies. It seems obvious that the word "secret" means "no intention to reveal this to unauthorized personnel." And Simus was a person who could impact the Russian position in these negotiations as well as the security of their operations.

Via radio, the Russian ship began to demand the return of the defecting sailor. Now Captain E. faced a far more serious situation. Not only was his crypto equipment down, he knew that the Russians would not stop until they had their crypto man back.

Captain E. was in his first command. Like many Coast Guard officers, he had high hopes for his future. All of his dreams were now in jeopardy. One wrong move, and his career would be over. It is worth noting at this time that a captain of a military vessel is, in most situations, the highest authority. This is what they are trained for; this is what they do. Wrong choices weed out those who will not reach the top.

Unsure as to how to proceed, Captain E. decided to contact the Coast Guard district headquarters in Boston. This was his fatal mistake: in not taking responsibility for his actions, he was illustrating his inability to command. Plus, because his crypto was not operational, all of the communications with District One went over open airwaves.

Chapter 15: Simus Kudirka

I had reboarded the Active (after my very short leave) by the time this had started to transpire, so I was able to listen in to what was taking place.

Captain E. did not know that the admiral of the district had gone home on sick leave. In his place was the admiral's adjutant, Captain X., who (like Captain E.) was leery of making the wrong decision. Captain X. called Washington, DC!

On this particular weekend, there were few high-ranking officials in Washington, DC (I can probably assume that this is most often the case). Instead of reaching the Secretary of State, Captain X. reached some undersecretary to the undersecretary of an undersecretary.

Just like on the Vigilant, in the first Coast Guard district office in Washington, DC, nobody wanted to make a decision. Still, Washington's suggestion was to give Simus back to the Russians. This was then relayed by Captain X. back to Captain E. (it's amazing how mistakes compound; one mistake generating two mistakes generating four mistakes generating eight mistakes, and so on).

Captain E. now realized his initial error, but there was no turning back. How do you give somebody back who has asked for asylum? If you try to drive him over, he's going to resist; if you tell him to go over alone, he'll refuse. There seemed to be no option that would work … so Captain E. called Captain X. again for advice.

Even after some consideration, Captain X. could not see a way through this without making matters worse. He called Washington once more to seek their advice.

The people in Washington were not military people. They had no understanding of the ramifications of the situation. To them it was simplistic; they suggested that if the defector couldn't be brought over by our men, they ought to let the Russians come to the cutter and retrieve him. At a loss as to what else to do, Captain X. relayed this information to Captain E.

This all happened while the Active was approaching the Cape Cod Canal. All of us in the radio room had difficulty believing our ears! Would the captain of a US military vessel really allow members of a foreign government onto that vessel to commit an act of violence? In any scenario this would be considered an act of war. Surely Captain

E. would never allow that to happen! But it had become apparent that Captain E. no longer had control of the situation.

We listened in shock as he radioed the Russian ship and told them that he would allow them to retrieve the sailor. A detachment of the KGB (which were assigned to every Russian ship) made their way in a small boat to the Vigilant.

Meanwhile the Russian defector was being entertained in the ward room. The ward room was located on the second deck and could be accessed through three doors and one hatch. That hatch opened onto the first deck, where there was a passageway along the side of the ship to the stern. This hatch was open in case of emergencies and was in the far corner of the wardroom.

When the KGB boarded, they were escorted to the rear door of the ward room. Once again I remind you that these were armed members of a foreign government who were about to commit an act of aggression on a US military vessel!

I have no doubt that because of Simus's role, he knew every KGB officer onboard his ship. When he saw those men enter the ward room, I don't know how long it took for him to react or what ran through his mind. I imagine that all of his hopes, all of his dreams, all of his visions of living in a free America vanished in instant.

What would you do in a similar situation? He did what was perhaps the only thing available to him: jump down through the hatch and run to the back of the vessel to try and swim for shore. Quite a few hours had passed since he first jumped to the deck of the cutter. It was apparent that if there were any pain left in his ankle, it was overridden by his adrenaline. Captain E. ordered the cutter underway immediately.

It is something to behold when a 210-foot cutter goes from stop to full speed. The hull can literally rise out of the water as it lunges forward. As Simus reached the stern, the crew at that location, who had no idea of what was transpiring, grabbed him to prevent him from jumping over the side. Though Simus spoke English, in his excitement he was screaming to be let free in Russian. None of the crew knew Russian, so they had no idea what he was saying. All they knew was that if he went over the side, the cutter propellers would kill him instantly; so they held onto him.

Chapter 15: Simus Kudirka

Shortly behind Simus were the KGB agents. By this time they had their weapons drawn. Captain E. did not want the Russians to do anything rash as most of his crew was unarmed. To prevent the situation from escalating, Captain E. immediately told all of his crew to stand down. He also stopped the engines again just in case.

The Russians proceeded to wrestle the defector to the deck and secure his arms and legs. They then dragged him toward their small boat that was tied alongside the Vigilant.

This was about the time that the Active appeared on the scene. After the beating and dragging, the defector appeared to be unconscious. We saw the KGB men throw Simus from the cutter's deck down to the waiting boat and return to the Russian mother ship. When they reached it, a rope was thrown over the side, tied to Simus's legs, and he was hauled aboard.

What a mess, and what a political disaster! In the days that followed more information about the young defector surfaced. It seemed that the young man's mother was a US citizen who had married a Russian. She had gone back to Lithuania to live with her husband and raise her child, Simus. Her Christianity and training had put hope in his heart. Her stories about freedom of religion (and freedom in general) in America had fueled his fire. Now that fire was out. Young Simus was off to exile in Siberia.

What a stern reminder to anyone else who wanted to try the same thing! What an effective propaganda tool. Let the young man live in prison in Siberia so that others would never try again! The most unfortunate part of that lesson was the message that if you did make it to America, Russia could still reach you. This made all the Russian sailors believe that their country was far more powerful than America.

Since all the transmissions had been over the open airwaves, the world also knew the story. Lithuanian society was incensed and demanded the immediate release of the defector. This became even more complicated when it was discovered that the defector's mother was a US citizen, which meant Simus himself had the option of receiving US citizenship!

The aftermath in America was huge. The entire crew of the Vigilant was restationed and replaced within thirty days. One of those crewmembers was actually transferred to the Active (I believe he suffered post-traumatic stress syndrome). Captain E. was transferred to Governors Island, New York (this is one of those dead-end positions). It signaled the end of his career, as Captain E., who was really a commander, would never receive any higher rank. He could only wait out his retirement. Captain X. in Washington would likewise never make Admiral. The dominoes fell, right down the line.

It took Secretary of State Henry Kissinger three years to secure the release of Simus Kudirka from Siberia. He would be shipped from Siberia to America via New York. Some mindless diplomat in Washington thought it would be good for the Coast Guard to welcome Simus to his new home. They did not realize that the base commander of Governors Island was the very man who had sent Simus back to the Russians!

How would you react if the first person you met when you came off of your plane to America was the one man that you should have hated above all other men? Matthew 5:43-45 says:

> You have heard that it was said, 'You shall love your neighbor and hate your enemy.' But I say to you, love your enemies, bless those who curse you, do good to those who hate you, and pray for those who spitefully use you and persecute you, that you may be sons of your Father in heaven; for He makes His sun rise on the evil and on the good, and sends rain on the just and on the unjust.

It is said that when Simus got off the plane in New York, he extended his hand to Captain E. and said, "My God tells me to forgive you, and that I am to bless and pray for you."

Simus was a Christian, and for all I know he still is. To have survived all that he experienced and to do what he did when he returned is one of the best definitions of faith I have ever seen.

Would your faith have enabled you to do this after being brutally beaten and dragged on the deck of a Coast Guard cutter? After three years of hard labor in Siberia? Would your faith have enabled you to do this even *without* all of those events?

Our commitment to Jesus Christ must be total. We need to be as secure in our faith as young Simus was in his.

CHAPTER 16:
HOLLY AND THE DOOR

For He shall give His angels charge over you, To keep you in all your ways. (Ps. 91:11)

Life onboard ship was a constant challenge. That being said, my wife Lorelei faced just as many of her own trials at home during that time. To start with, she was dealing with a one-year-old and pregnant with our second. Unfortunately, I was in port only three to four days a month.

We were living in an apartment building in Rye, New Hampshire, just ten minutes from the ship's dock. The only entrance to our unit was in the kitchen. The porch there had an overhang which was connected to the garages; garages which were in the process of being torn down. Holly, our first child, was just beginning to walk, and she enjoyed going to the screen door and watching all of the activity.

One day Lorelei was at the sink, about ten feet away from Holly, when our daughter reached up and pushed the screen door open. At once she "stepped down," or sort of fell forward. She was not able to step back up to get in.

Just as Holly went out, there was an awful cracking noise. Lorelei heard it but was unable to react. As she looked over, she saw Holly fly headfirst into the kitchen a foot above the floor! This all happened within seconds as the roof came crashing down.

> *Just as Holly went out, there was an awful cracking noise. Lorelei heard it but was unable to react.*

Most of the garages had already been removed, but the workmen had failed to support the overhang above our porch. They had been taking a break and had seen Holly fall forward onto the porch. After the collapse they came running, hollering frantically, thinking she was under the rubble.

Lorelei hollered back, saying, "She is all right! She is in here, safe."

The workmen were shaken, as they had been sure Holly was buried in the rubble. They confessed to Lorelei that the landlord told them to make sure they supported the roof before detaching it from the garage.

"It is a miracle" they said.

Albert Einstein once said, "Coincidence is God's way of remaining anonymous." Our angels do not take breaks! They are ever-watching. Nothing happens by chance or without their knowledge.

CHAPTER 17: TRANSFER TO ALASKA

Mark the blameless *man*, and observe the upright; for the future of *that* man *is* peace. But the transgressors shall be destroyed together; the future of the wicked shall be cut off. But the salvation of the righteous *is* from the Lord; *He is* their strength in the time of trouble. And the Lord shall help them and deliver them; He shall deliver them from the wicked, and save them, because they trust in Him. (Ps. 37:37-40)

God knows the beginning from the end and sees the greater picture. We, on the other hand, have a small view of the events in this world, including those in our own lives. As He is directing our steps, it is sometimes hard for us to understand why He's chosen the particular path He is using.

Someone once said that faith is taking the next step without seeing the whole staircase. Because hindsight is often 20/20, although we cannot see the direct hand of God in most cases in the moment, we can yet see the shadow of the work He has done.

Chapter 17: Transfer to Alaska

In a previous story I told how I had escaped court-martial during my time at Eaton's Neck. You'll recall how, in the end, a number of officers and warrant officers were either forced to retire or received reprimands. You would think that that was the end of the story, but as I mentioned before, it was just beginning.

After the actions of the federal judge, we finally felt that the issue was over. Life could now return to some form of normalcy; we could move forward.

Life has a way of taking detours.

Shortly after those events, a man came to visit the Eaton's Neck Coast Guard station. He was a chief electronics technician like me, and since he was from the area, he wanted to see what the station was like.

I learned that he had had orders to report for isolated duty in Alaska, but before he could leave they had been changed. While waiting for his new orders, he was home visiting family and friends on Long Island.

I found it interesting that the station he had been on was one that my brother-in-law had been at just three years earlier: Cape Sarichef, Alaska. I also felt somehow uneasy after talking with him. I wondered why his orders had been changed. I soon got my answer when I received orders for that same LORAN station.

LORAN stands for long range aids to navigation. This system was used in a series of remote transmitting sites for ship and air navigation before GPS satellites. A site consisted of a main transmitting station and two substations, the triangulation of which would give a fairly accurate position for a vessel with the right equipment.

Because of the intensity of the transmitting signal and the geographical area that they covered, most stations were in remote locations. One substation was on Unimak Island, which was at the beginning of the Aleutian chain. Unimak Island was totally uninhabited except for two stations: the Coast Guard navigation station, populated by about forty support personnel, and a White Alice telephone relay station, about five miles away from the first station and consisting of six civilian employees.

It was unusual to receive orders for isolated duty when those orders would extend beyond your normal enlistment, and a normal tour of duty on Unimak Island would be longer than I had already been at Eaton's Neck. However, it appeared that I would be required to attend special LORAN school training then spend at least one year on station. This process would keep me active well past my release date.

I took note that the chief of personnel of the Coast Guard, Captain F., was one of those who had received a reprimand during the court-martial ordeal. This very same captain had originally stationed me at Eaton's Neck. He had also been the commander of Group Long Island Sound when I first arrived there (my wife had a run in with him that he will never forget, but that is yet another story, perhaps for another book!). Finally, this captain was known to have a very close relationship with CWO-4 Sam, the commanding officer of the station at Eaton's Neck (who had been asked to retire early).

You did not have to be the brightest bulb on the Christmas tree to see the connection, not to mention to realize the potential hardship this would create for my family and for my separation from the Coast Guard. I called the placement office in Washington, DC, and informed them that I had no intentions of re-enlisting. The orders stood.

There are ways of punishing without officially punishing, and I felt that this fit into that category. My first stop was the federal judge who had helped me before, but he told me there was nothing he could do regarding something of this nature. He suggested that I contact the civil rights officer of the third Coast Guard district.

This just happened to be Captain B., whom I had met during that memorable lifeboat station inspection. He immediately saw the injustice of what was taking place. In the end, however, he discovered that the orders had come from way above his pay grade: the admiral of the third district himself.

Once again I had not learned my lesson to start with God instead of saving God as my last resort. I now called Pastor Nick and sought his advice.

He suggested that we contact an Adventist congressman from California who had significant contacts. He might help to resolve the situation. We compiled a letter listing all the facts, the results of the different actions, and the new pseudo-punishment.

Chapter 17: Transfer to Alaska

After talking with the congressman, he agreed to address the situation in Washington. He said that he was going to be dealing with the commandant of the Coast Guard directly. Once again I felt that the issue would be resolved. A few days later I received a call from the placement captain himself.

When I answered the phone, his first words were, "Your white knight is gone, and you will be in Alaska in four weeks." I recognized Captain F.'s voice before he gave me his name. He proceeded to inform me that the congressman would not be able to assist me in any way.

Eventually I heard that the congressman had died in a plane crash. I also later found out that the captain of the Coast Guard cutter Dallas, who had been the captain of the Active when I first reported to that ship, had requested that I be transferred to his new command in New York City. But the admiral of the third Coast Guard district had flatly refused to have me remain in his district. There was no chance that anyone would stop the inevitable.

During these efforts I had been attending LORAN school in New York City while still stationed at Eaton's Neck, Long Island. I had just completed the training when I received that final phone call. Like I said, my enlistment should have been up by this time; but a person can be held involuntarily well beyond his normal discharge date.

Lorelei and I resigned ourselves to the year of separation that was to come. We now had to determine where our family was going to live during that period, because they could not come to an isolated station with me.

Because of my rank, the Coast Guard had to move my family anywhere I wanted within the forty-eight contiguous states. By now I had decided that at the end of this assignment I would leave the service. I had also decided that I would attend Andrews University in Berrien Springs, Michigan. For these reasons, I figured, why not have the Coast Guard move my family to Berrien Springs before my final tour in Alaska?

It sounded like a reasonable idea. The problem was that we had no house or apartment in the Michigan area, and we had only three weeks to secure one.

I contacted the moving company and arranged for them to pack my goods that week. It took about one day to pack and load the truck, after which they asked what the destination was for delivery. I told him that it would be Berrien Springs, Michigan, but I did not have a location as of yet.

They informed me that if they did not have a location before they left, all my goods would go into storage. Plus, the process of getting them released and moved into my home or apartment would take about three weeks. At best, this would mean that my wife and two small girls (four and five years old) would still be without furniture for at least one week after I had gone to Alaska! Still, we could see no way around this, so we decided to go to Michigan.

When I was signed out from my duties at the Eaton's Neck Coast Guard station, I was given my personnel file, health file, and payroll file to hand-carry to my new station. They also included my pay for the three weeks before I left for Alaska.

After getting back to the empty house and reviewing all that I had received, I realized that I had been overpaid by $250. I called the district office, and they told me they would deduct the money from my next check or from the money that I would be getting in Alaska (which would be separate from Lorelei's allotment).

I told them to send all the money to my wife, because I did not think there would be any use for money on an isolated station in the middle of nowhere! Whatever extra there would be could be better-used by her.

With papers in hand, we loaded the car with our suitcases, the girls, and our Saint Bernard. With not an inch of space left over, we headed for Michigan.

I had planned on a few days in a motel until such time as we could locate an apartment or house. What I had not expected was to be unable to find an apartment or house at all! We checked the newspaper and every bulletin board we could find, but to no avail. Someone suggested contacting a real estate agent, saying they sometimes handled rental properties. The person wrote down a name and number, and I called and scheduled an appointment.

I'm not saying I make a habit of misplacing notes, but when the afternoon came, this note was nowhere to be found!

I can remember numbers: the serial number of my M1 in boot camp, my social security number, my wife's social security number, my

Chapter 17: Transfer to Alaska

kids' social security numbers, pi to the seventh place … the list goes on. But could I remember that seven-digit phone number?

And the name? Those had always been difficult for me. If everyone had a number instead, life would be so much simpler! What I did remember was that the real estate agent's name began with a K.

I figured there couldn't be too many agents in the small town of Berrien Springs whose names began with K. The plan was to drive into town and look for a match. Not a great plan; but we figured it would work in Berrien Springs.

As we came into town, I saw a sign for Ketchiklo Real Estate. Even if this was not the correct place, he would probably know all of the other agents in town, or else he might be able to help me directly.

I walked in the door and saw a man behind a desk speaking on the telephone. If there's one thing the military does correctly, it teaches you to have respect. I stood in front of his desk at attention, waiting for him to finish.

He put his hand over the mouthpiece and looked at me. I expected him to say, "I'll be with you in a minute." Instead he asked me if I was from New England.

I thought this was a bit strange. I was not sure whether I was dressed differently or just looked different than the people in the Midwest. I answered him, "Yes."

He went back to listening on the phone, then once again put his hand over the mouthpiece, looked up at me, and asked me if I had two children.

Starting to feel just a little bit strange, once again I answered, "Yes."

He continued to listen on the phone, then covered the mouthpiece for a third time. Again he looked up at me. This time he asked if I was going to be attending Andrews University.

Now I was not planning on *immediately* going to the university, but I would be attending once I returned from my station in Alaska. I did not feel it was wrong to once again say, "Yes."

He listened some more, and one final time he put his hand over the mouthpiece. He asked me if I was looking for a place to rent.

By now I was feeling very uneasy, but for the fourth time I said, "Yes."

The man behind the desk told the person on the phone that he was sending somebody over. Then he hung up, handed me an address, and told me the landlord would be waiting for me at that location.

When I returned to the car, Lorelei asked me if I had had any luck. I handed her the address and told her what I had had to do to get it: say yes four times!

The address was an old farmhouse in the town of Buchanan. It was just outside of town and easily within commuting distance of the university. It was also located on a quiet dirt road across from another farm and a few small houses. The farmhouse had a small shed, a corn crib, and a large barn, together forming a beautiful, U-shaped collection of buildings nestled in 300 acres of corn and soybeans.

We met the landlord, and as we toured the farmhouse, we realized that this was far more than we had ever asked for. It had two stories, five bedrooms, a root cellar, and was an ideal place to raise two small children. But I had not talked to the real estate agent back in town about how much I could afford, and I had no clue as to what rents were in this area. This place would probably be outside of our means.

> *Our potential landlord asked me a question that in all my years of renting I have never been asked: how much I could afford!*

Our potential landlord turned to me and asked me a question that in all my years of renting I have never been asked: how much I could afford!

Not knowing where to go with this, I responded as honestly as I could, based on rents that we had paid in the past (but also based on much smaller places). I told him that I was hoping to find a place for about $150 per month, all the time knowing that this was probably a fraction of what his place went for.

He looked at me, smiled, and said that this was exactly how much he was looking for. Furthermore, he would not require an advance month's rent or deposit (you don't have to convince me that God works in mysterious ways His wonders to perform!). The landlord then said that there was just one more thing. I knew that it was too good to be true!

Chapter 17: Transfer to Alaska

With my daughters in front of our miracle Michigan rental. God is good!

He told me they had just filled the double oil tanks outside, and I would have to pay for my own fuel. This meant that I would have to reimburse him for the fuel they had just put in. When he told me that the cost came to $250, I almost fell over, since I had $250 more in my budget that I had planned on having available.

When God says He directs our steps, this is not figurative. It is quite literal, and we should not be surprised when situations like this happen. As Proverbs 3:5 and 6 says, "Trust in the Lord with all your heart, and lean not on your own understanding; in all your ways acknowledge Him, and He shall direct your paths."

It was no coincidence that I lost the name Kiefer and found the *other* agent whose name began with K in the small town of Berrien Springs. It was not a coincidence that I was overpaid $250. But what about that phone call? What was that all about?

Later on, after my tour in Alaska, I had the opportunity to ask our landlord what had actually happened. He told me that after reading

Yankee magazine, he had had a dream in which he was told to rent his farmhouse to a man from New England who had two children and was going to attend the university!

He was not of my faith, but he was a Christian. This dream had bothered him, so he had called his realtor. He had begun explaining the dream to him, and for some unknown reason the realtor would stop him from time to time and talk to somebody else. When he was done relating the dream, the realtor had said that he had somebody for the landlord to meet and was sending the man over to the farmhouse.

My landlord had made that telephone call at the same time that I was in the realtor's office. Can we ever doubt, can we ever question the wonder of our Lord?

Some thirty-seven years later, we met a person that knew our landlord. At that time we put this story down in a letter to pass along to that wonderful man. I pray that it had as powerful an effect on him as those events had on our lives. But I digress: the story is not finished.

We now had a house that was completely empty: not a stitch of furniture in the entire place, nothing except for our suitcases and two small children running from room to room listening to the wonderful echoes.

There were two bedrooms on the main floor; one for my wife and one for the two girls. The Saint Bernard had his own private quarters on the side of the corn crib that he seemed to enjoy greatly. Thus, since I would be gone for nearly a year, we decided it would be best to close the second floor completely.

You will recall that the movers had informed us when they took our goods from New York that it would take three weeks to have them delivered to us from the storage facility. Yet I had to leave for Alaska in *one* week. This meant that Lorelei and the girls would be sleeping on the floor for some time.

Since we did not have a phone yet, I went to the nearest payphone (yes, they did have those back then) and called the moving company. I was prepared to beg, grovel, and do whatever I needed to do to get our furniture as soon as possible.

The mover said that he needed to check the files. I waited while I heard the sound of rustling paper in the background. Then there came an, "Oh, my!"

Somehow those words aren't always comforting. As I waited for him to pick the phone back up, all kinds of scenarios ran through my mind. Not a one of them was anywhere close to the reality that unfolded.

When the mover returned to the phone, he said, "It looks like we have good news and bad news."

I told him to give me the bad news first. I don't know why it always seems easier to take the bad news first and then follow with whatever the good is, but that's how I am.

He told me that the storage house they had planned to place our belongings in had burned to the ground.

My heart sunk to about three feet below the floor. That's tough to do when you're in a cement-bottomed phone booth!

Then he continued, "The good news is that we were never able to get your goods off of the moving truck. We have been unable to locate an open storage facility to place your belongings in, so is there any way that you can receive the furniture tomorrow?"

I did not know whether to cry, to laugh, to drop the phone and pray, or to step outside of the booth and just scream, "Thank you, God!"

Many times in my stories, I have said I do not believe in coincidence. Now you begin to understand why. To simply say that we serve an awesome God somehow is just not good enough.

CHAPTER 18: COLD IS A STATE OF MIND

God *is* our refuge and strength, a very present help in trouble. Therefore we will not fear, even though the earth be removed, and though the mountains be carried into the midst of the sea; *though* its waters roar *and* be troubled, *though* the mountains shake with its swelling. *Selah* (Ps. 46:1-3)

People chuckle when I tell them that cold is a state of mind, but the human body is capable of enduring tremendous cold and tremendous adversity. And we can also endure when we understand that God is our refuge and strength; a very present help in time of trouble.

God tells us in 2 Chronicles 7:14, "If My people who are called by My name will humble themselves, and pray and seek My face, and turn from their wicked ways, then I will hear from heaven, and will forgive their sin and heal their land." Prayer doesn't answer the question. It *is* the answer!

Chapter 18: Cold is a State of Mind

This next story touches upon the limits of endurance and the need for prayer.

On the far side of Unimak Island in the Aleutian chain, there is a point of land called Scotch Cap. On this point of land there is an automated lighthouse, the purpose of which is to be a beacon for the entrance into the shipping lanes of North Alaska.

There was a time when this lighthouse was manned by five coast guardsmen. Shortly after World War II, in 1946, they had just finished rebuilding the station house. The house was built on the side of a cliff, about eighty feet away from the water and another sixty feet above the landing. They used a new technology called ferroconcrete; a process in which rebar, or iron rods, are placed inside the concrete to greatly increase the strength and durability of that material. Like the Titanic, they said that the new station house could withstand anything. They could not have been more wrong.

On April 1, 1946, there was an earthquake on Unimak. Warning of a possible tsunami was radioed to the small Coast Guard lighthouse.

Contrary to movies and popular belief, tidal waves travel underwater. As one approaches shore, the sea bottom will force the wave up to its full height. Unimak Island is of volcanic origin; for this reason, the ocean floor drops to almost 1,000 feet within a few hundred feet from shore. This sharp drop meant that the station would have virtually no warning whatsoever when the tidal wave arrived.

On that fateful day, a 100-foot wave hit the small building. To the amazement of all, the building held. The crew cheered.

However, it is not unusual for the second wave to be larger than the first. So it was on that April Fools' Day in 1946.

They later estimated the second wave to have been nearly 180 feet high. It finally broke nearly a quarter-mile inland. As the wave retreated, it took the entire station and building, along with its inhabitants, out to sea. The first time that I saw the remains of the original structure, after I arrived on Unimak for my assignment, I was in awe at the power of the ocean.

The station was rebuilt beyond the edges of the cliff, and an unmanned light structure was attached. It became the responsibility of the Coast Guard base at Cape Sarichef to maintain the light, the generators, and the fuel transfer necessary to ensure that navigational aid continued.

To accomplish this, once a month a small crew went over a fourteen-mile stretch to the remote site at Scotch Cap. Fourteen miles may not seem like a very long distance, but considering the conditions, the average trip took twenty-four hours!

There were two possible vehicles to use. The first was the Thiokol, a fully-tracked vehicle with five tires on each side controlling the track. It was driven much like a bulldozer or tank. If you have ever driven a snowmobile, you would love to drive one of these! The advantage of this vehicle was its ability to travel over snow. The disadvantage was its inability to traverse open cold lava fields. Lava rock is a lot like glass and just as sharp, so there was a real possibility of puncturing the tires and throwing a track. If you threw a track, you were dead in place.

The second vehicle was called a Unimog. It had massive, six-foot tires, thirty-two forward gears, and sixteen reverse. It was a lot like driving a semi-tractor trailer and was also loads of fun. I once had the

Our hardy Thiokol, capable of handling (almost) anything Alaska threw at us.

Chapter 18: Cold is a State of Mind

opportunity to race a D5 bulldozer in one of those babies. The weakness of this vehicle was snow: one could drive through five feet of mud and not stop, but for some reason five feet of snow was its downfall.

One day I was taking crewmen to Scotch Cap to refuel the site and fix the radio telemetry between the two stations. We had recently received about ten feet of snow, and before setting out we received warning of another possible storm. The snow was a real problem, but weather could not be a factor; the light had to be maintained.

We assumed that snow covered the entire fourteen miles, so even though the wind was strong, we decided to take the tracked vehicle. And if something bad happened on the way, every five miles on the way to the station was a survival shelter which consisted of an 8' x 8' steel plate box with a hatch on top (the reason they had hatches rather than doors was because of the lovely, cuddly, and cute sixteen-foot Kodiak brown bears that shared the island with us). Inside each box there were MRE meals and blankets.

So four of us started the journey in temperatures that approached 75 degrees below zero. For those that are not sure how cold this is, if you took a thermos full of water and threw the water into the air, it would freeze solid before it hit the ground. And let me assure you: temperatures of minus 30 degrees and lower feel about the same. Any exposed skin will instantly freeze.

> *The storm was too severe for them to come, let alone to be able to find us. We would have to wait*

The nice thing about wind chill, however, is that it only affects people or animals. As long as we stayed in the vehicle, it was no colder than our heater allowed it to be. Even without a heater, it would have been no colder than the static temperature (that is, the temperature minus any wind chill effect).

The downside to this storm was that visibility was about twenty feet! Everything was white; we had to crawl so that we didn't run off the edge of a cliff.

We were about three-quarters of the way to Scotch Cap when we saw that the wind had cleared the lava flats of snow for about a half-mile stretch. We were already twenty hours from the home station, and we were sure that we could make it across, so we decided to move forward.

The first quarter-mile went fairly well. Then we heard a loud *pop!* We had just lost one of the tires on one side of the vehicle. But there were four more tires supporting that track, so we continued.

In a matter of just a few more feet, we heard several more *pops*. We realized that we had two tires left on one side and three on the other. The danger we now faced was breaking the track! Fresh tires could be provided, but replacing a *track* at this remote location would have been very, very difficult. We got on the radio and contacted our base for a relay to the nearest base that could help us. That was Kodiak, Alaska. We asked for a C-130 aircraft to airdrop us replacement tires.

The response we got was not what we had hoped for: the storm was too severe for them to come, let alone to be able to find us. We would have to wait until the storm had passed, and unfortunately we were not near a survival shelter.

We knew that we could not wait inside the vehicle. We also knew that we could not keep the radio on indefinitely, because the battery would not survive. Just a hundred feet away, we could see the snow again. It appeared to be about ten feet deep. We had been taught how to build an emergency shelter, so if we could make it to the snow, with four bodies we would be able to warm up the inside to a balmy zero degrees.

We all had some type of foul weather gear. I was wearing a snowmobile suit that I had brought from Michigan (it ended up lasting me until about 2010, at which time we gave it an appropriate burial). Before leaving the vehicle, we contacted Kodiak one more time and told them that every twelve hours, we would check in to find out the status.

This meant two of us would have to leave our shelter and come back to the vehicle, start it, and charge the batteries so that the radio could be used (two of us, as we always worked in pairs for safety). We would walk hand over hand, following a rope we would lay out from the vehicle to our camp.

Once the storm was in full force, one misstep could lead you into a frozen world of no return! You would not be able to hear, see, or sense more than a foot ahead of you, and with a static temperature of about

Chapter 18: Cold is a State of Mind 99

minus 40, the wind chill approached minus 75! Now you can begin to understand why I tell people that cold is a state of mind! So that small cord became our safety connection to our partner and survival.

We proceeded to the snow bank and built our shelter. That was step number one. Step number two consisted of setting up a watch, for if all of us went to sleep at once, there was a good possibility that no one would wake up! One of us had to be awake at all times, and watches were about six hours long. At the end of each period, the watchman would wake up his replacement, then check the breathing of all the other crewmen before settling in for his own nap. After two watches it would be time to contact Kodiak.

Each time we called, they told us what we already knew: the storm was still raging. This continued for one day, then two days, then three days, then four, five, six, and finally a seventh day. I always found it just a little bit ironic that it took seven days for the storm to break. We had left on a Sunday, and our deliverance came on the Sabbath!

The engine compartment of that little vehicle could be accessed from inside the Thiokol. During our wait we were able to melt snow to provide small amounts water. Our rations, however, were gone by the second day, so the last five days were hungry ones.

On the seventh day, we heard the engine of the C-130 (it's amazing how that huge aircraft can still stay in the air moving only sixty miles an hour). The sky was now clear, and they found us without any difficulty.

As it flew over on the first pass, I know the pilot would have programmed the plane's course into the computer. On the second pass, we saw the entire crew at the rear of the aircraft pushing out a bundle of tires as they passed overhead. After watching them bounce for a while, we collected the tires and repaired our vehicle.

All we had to do now was pray that we could make it across that last stretch without popping another tire ... which we did. The rest of the journey to the station was without incident.

One more interesting situation took place on that trip, at the Scotch Cap fuel tanks. It consisted of a large, male, fifteen-foot-tall Kodiak brown bear taking a nap between them. Since we had to access those tanks, we had to first find a way to encourage the bear to leave.

When you are on top of the food chain, there are not many things that will scare you. First, we tried yelling. Then we fired a number of

Bear Cliff, Scotch Cap. Named in honor of a certain daredevil.

rounds into the air with our M-16s. I stayed at the vehicle while the other three men fanned out. We hoped that the bear would take the hint.

As he stood and stretched, we realized that the only ones who needed to take a hint were us. I'm not sure whether he just decided he didn't want to deal with us, or if he didn't like the sound of the guns, but he turned and walked toward the edge of the cliff.

I think it was about that time that we realized that the only way he could escape would be to go through us. This would not be a good situation. We watched as he looked over his shoulder ... then looked out over the cliff ... then, in an instant, we saw him leap!

We rushed to the edge and saw him land some sixty feet below on the beach, rise, and slowly walk away! The Kodiak brown bear is yet another one of God's amazing creatures.

Thankfully, on the way back to Sarichef, we found a way to circumnavigate the lava field and thus avoid having a return incident.

The one thing that kept our sanity in that snowstorm was our radio connection with the base and Kodiak. The cord also helped us realize that we had to always stay connected.

The one thing that can keep our sanity in this world is our connection through prayer with our loving Father. God is our refuge and strength and our ever-present help in times of trouble. There is no place on this earth He cannot hear us or see us. There is no trial so severe that He cannot help us overcome.

CHAPTER 19: THOMAS

Judge not, that you be not judged. For with what judgment you judge, you will be judged; and with the measure you use, it will be measured back to you. (Matt. 7:1, 2)

Despite God's admonition about judging others, it seems to be the one thing that we do the most of in this world (today we have renamed it discrimination). We judge by size, race, intelligence, language, and even gender. There appears to be nothing that we can't use to feel better than somebody else about. But the method that seems to irritate me the most is *judging*.

In this next account, I feel that I did not do what I should have done in the beginning. I therefore share responsibility for what happened. It is as important to stand for your principles as it is to have them. We may not be judging others ourselves, but if we do not stand up for those who cannot stand up for themselves, we are, in effect, enabling others to judge.

Chapter 19: Thomas

I knew that most of the men on that isolated post on Unimak Island were there because they had offended someone or just made too many waves. Not in every case, but the majority of the personnel assigned to this station were there to resolve an unwanted situation.

The chief whom I had replaced, for example, had been on the island for over two years. He was assigned the post because, near the end of the Vietnam War, he had witnessed a major mistake. The small river patrol craft that he was on was cut in half by our own Air Force; a case of friendly fire. The war was winding down, and the powers that be wanted to keep the entire incident quiet. That's why they had transferred the poor man to this island, where there was little to no communication with the outside world.

Now I wasn't complaining, because there are worse stations I could have been sent to: such as French Frigate Shoals, which is halfway between Midway and the Pacific Rim, or Cape Atholl, located nearly 1,000 miles north of Thule, Greenland).

But why Tom was sent here directly from boot camp, I will never understand. Tom was a quiet and shy, seventeen-year-old African-American boy. Born and raised in the country, he had never had to experience the fight for survival of living in a city environment. And never having been away from home, he had walked into a cruel world that was blind to innocence.

I do know that he was having a terrible time adjusting to a station consisting of several redneck coasties! There were plenty of signs to show that he was not dealing with the stress and was struggling to just exist. And as the executive officer of the station, I was in a position to stop all the hazing and harassment of poor Tom.

I tried my best to make friends with him, and I did prevent anything physical from happening, but mental abuse can be just as debilitating and leaves just as many scars. Only after the situation had developed did I realize that being someone's friend is more than just holding their hand. It is standing up for them when others move in on them.

Meanwhile life went on. We all lived on a rock in the middle of nowhere. We were dependent on supply deliveries once every couple of months, which meant that our mail, our perishable goods, and those sweet treats from home were few and far between. And most all of our meals came from a can, while what fresh meat they had was terrible.

Three years before I arrived on the station, the storekeeper had ordered minute steaks which consisted of shaved beef. The problem was that instead of ordering 500 pounds, he had ordered 5,000 … and we were still 2,000 pounds shy of finishing up on his mistake. The other unfortunate aspect of this error was that he had utilized all of our meat quotas for several years. We were destined to either enjoy minute steak or hunt our own caribou. I don't think there is a single way you can prepare minute steaks that was not tried by our cook!

More on supplies. Like I said in an earlier story, a couple of miles from our station there was a White Alice radio transmitting relay link. That station was owned and operated by AT&T and had a crew of six civilian employees. Each of those civilian employees drew a six-figure income, and if they stayed on the site for more than 360 days, they would receive their salary tax-free, courtesy of some lobbyist deal in Washington. The other perk that they received was regular flights that brought fresh supplies.

Crazy Dave, the pilot who brought me to the island (and let me state that he earned his name), made those regular trips for AT&T. It was actually because of one of his flights that I was able to get to the island despite the weather.

On one particular excursion, he brought their staff a fresh supply of produce, vegetables, and milk; all the sort of things those of us at the Coast Guard station had not seen in quite some time. The head of that little station invited the commanding officer and I to a special dinner which would include fresh salad and fresh vegetables. How could we refuse?

Knowing that we would be there for several hours, we had one of the crew drive us to the little hill where the White Alice site was located. We chatted with the station head for about an hour and were just getting ready to sit down to our beautiful dinner when we heard a Jeep beeping and racing up to the site.

The duty driver ran into the dining hall and informed us that Tom had gone over the edge. He had gotten hold of an M-16 and was threatening to kill every man on the station. He had even fired some shots into the ceiling of the main reception area.

The CO looked at me. I nodded my head, and we both ran for the Jeep. As soon as we arrived back at our station, I jumped out. As I was

Chapter 19: Thomas

the closest to the doors, I ran into the vestibule, and as the outside door shut, I heard a gunshot. Then I realized that I would have to go in alone before those outside could enter.

It might be interesting to note that the entrance to the Coast Guard station was a series of doors forming an airlock. The outside door would open first, then it had to close behind you. The vestibule would be filled with warm air, and then finally the inside door could open. This was a safety feature to prevent all the warmth inside the building from being sucked out by the extreme cold outside.

When the inside door released, I ran in, not knowing where Tom might be by this time. It did not take me long to find out, as the terrified young man stuck the barrel of the M-16 in my face, just inches from my nose. I looked behind me and realized that nobody else was coming through the door. They could see what was happening from outside.

They must have then run around to the rear door because I saw them disappear. I turned back to look at Tom. A quick glance at the side of the M-16 told me that the weapon was in full automatic ... and his finger was on the trigger. One slip of that trigger finger, and everything north of my neck would be toast!

I could also see that Tom was shaking and crying. Because he was in a pretty unstable state, my first mission was to calm him down; that is, if I could keep myself calm! If ever there was a time for prayer, this was it.

> *His finger was on the trigger. One slip of that trigger finger, and everything north of my neck would be toast!*

After first talking with God, I turned to Tom. In as soothing a voice as I could muster, I told him to just relax and lower the weapon. It seemed the stupidest thing to say under the circumstances that I could possibly have come up with, but for some reason that's all I could do.

Tom was sobbing. He just kept saying over and over, "It's too late. It's too late!"

"Tom," I said, "it is not too late. Just relax, be careful, and for goodness' sake, take your finger off of the trigger!"

He at least did that much, but he still held the gun point-blank on my face. I knew that there was no way that I could make any move faster than his finger. We stood there and talked for twenty-five minutes, then thirty-five. Still there was no resolution in sight. What could I say to Tom to get him to stand down?

Finally I asked him what would he do, or what would he want, if this morning had never happened.

He looked at me and told me, "But it has, and there's no turning back!"

Again I said, "But what if it never happened: could you turn back then?"

Now he looked confused. "How could that ever be?" he said and looked up at the holes in the ceiling, then at the crew watching us through the different entrances.

"Well, Tom, let me put it this way. The only things that happen on this station are the things that get reported. If something is not reported, then in effect it never happened."

He thought for a second, then he asked if I could do that.

I answered, "Not only can I do that, I *would* do that. Now, I am not telling you that there are no consequences, as we will get you help. But they do not need to know what transpired before we ask for help for you, so this does not have to go on your record." As I said this, my thoughts went back to my start on the cutter Active and to how that captain had given me a second chance.

Tom still looked puzzled. He said, "I don't think you can do that."

I answered, "I can and I will."

Tom finally realized that I meant to do exactly what I said. He started to sob once again. At the same time, he lowered the M-16 and passed it to me.

I immediately dropped the clip, removed the round in the chamber, and broke down the gun so that it was unusable. Before the pieces hit the floor, the room was filled with armed men ready to take Tom into restraints.

The commanding officer came in. He was about to give the order to have Tom thrown in the brig when I motioned to him. I told the crew to hold Tom there until the commanding officer and I had had a chance to talk. The CO looked perplexed but followed me into his office.

After I shut the door, he asked what this was about. I explained the promise that I had made to Tom. The CO looked at me with a surprised expression and stated that we couldn't do that.

I very calmly asked him, "Why?"

He thought for a moment and answered, "I don't know."

I explained to him what I had explained to Tom: that the only things that officially happened were those things which we acknowledged. If we did not acknowledge anything as having happened today (that is, if we did not record them in the logs), then in effect those events had not happened.

I acknowledged that we needed to get Tom psychiatric help as soon as possible, and told him that I had explained to Tom that we intended to do just that, but I also reiterated that we did not have to tell all the reasons why we were seeking this help.

After a brief discussion, we decided to call immediately for a helicopter to come and take Tom to Kodiak station. They had medical and psychiatric facilities that could deal with Tom's issues. The only thing that we told them was that Tom was unable to deal with either the isolation or the separation from his family.

The helicopter arrived within twenty-four hours, and Tom never returned to Cape Sarichef. We were later informed that he spent several months at Kodiak, then went on to advanced training and eventually Officer Candidate School.

We all have gone to the point of no return in this world. We are told that all have sinned and fallen short of the glory of God (Rom. 3:23). But despite that short-falling, Jesus has promised to wipe our slate clean; to make it as if our sins had never happened.

This is one step beyond forgiving, because in making it as if it never happened, we can enjoy the life God originally intended for us to have: that is, as children of the King.

Our sin will not only be forgiven, it will be removed from us as far as it is from the mountains to the sea; never to be exposed again and virtually as if our sins never existed. Yet to have this happen in our lives, we must first accept the gift that Jesus has offered us!

With Tom, much of what transpired could have been avoided had I been more proactive in defending him. Still, nothing happens by chance. There is a plan for every person. I realize that the way things happen is because of God's plan, not mine.

I often wondered if his experience at Unimak and the grace that Tom received that day made him a better officer then he would have been otherwise. I still wish that I could have been more proactive. In the future I will be more aware of my part.

Our job in this world is not only to give grace but to raise the downtrodden, care about the abused, and love all.

CHAPTER 20: THE TOW LINE

But the end of all things is at hand; therefore be serious and watchful in your prayers. (1 Peter 4:7)

Long before Alaska, on a ship patrol after a fairly serious storm, we came upon two vessels that were disabled. Both were without power and neither was in good enough shape to deal with the condition of the sea.

Both fishing vessels were larger than 50-foot and had fairly heavy loads in their holds. Since we were more than 250 miles from the coast, it would have been impractical to take one back and return for the other. In fact, at a safe towing speed of about 15 knots, it would take several days just to deliver one ship and return.

The decision was made to put the vessels in tandem. This meant we would connect one line between the two vessels and then a towline to our stern. The largest towing hawser we had onboard was about six inches in diameter. Because there is no such thing as a line that cannot be broken, it was common practice with any hawser to place a length of small cord with a loop in it on the line, which let us determine how much the hawser was being stretched. This we did.

Towing two large vessels with so much weight onboard would restrict us to about ten knots. We would also have to maintain a close watch in the rough seas to prevent any vessel from being swamped and also to keep an eye on the towline.

I don't know if any of you have ever seen a nylon hawser break, but the amount of force that is released is beyond what you can imagine. We have all perhaps played with rubber bands, shooting them at each other, or made a whip with a piece of rope. The loud crack that you hear as you flick a rope is like the sound of a BB in comparison to a snapping hawser, which is like a cannon being fired!

So the towline was set, and a watch was established. The job was not to look around but rather only to monitor the little piece of string stitched across a two-foot section of the hawser, just beyond the cleat and a few feet from the fantail, or stern, of the ship.

The stern was just below the flight deck, which overlapped most of the stern. This gave some protection, but not a lot, from the driving rain.

Try standing a watch outside in rough weather in the middle of the night with no distractions (that is, no sounds other than the engines' monotonous drone). Add in the smell of diesel fuel and blowing rain. You have here a formula for fatigue. It was a struggle not just to watch that small loop in the cord but to even stay awake.

Fortunately it was not my duty. I had finished my own 4 p.m. to 8 p.m. watch on the bridge and had retired for the evening to get ready for my 3:30 a.m. wake-up call.

At about 2 a.m. the seas started to get a little heavier. The officer on deck decided to try to increase speed by five knots (to fifteen knots total), since there was another storm approaching and we were still 100 miles from our port of destination. After running at this increased speed a while, the strain on the towline began to show. The loop was now just below the hawser! We were nearing its maximum stretch point.

Chapter 20: The Tow Line

The US Coast Guard cutter Active (aft view of the flight deck overhanging the hawser locker).

The young fellow on watch then decided it was time for a cup of coffee. He stepped ten feet away from his post into the aft hawser locker. The locker (the same one that several years earlier I had so dutifully cleaned with a toothbrush) was just behind the cleat to which the towing line was secured. Its steel door was tied back, exposing the small room. Its coffee pot, set up for the man on watch, was just behind where the door was secured and thus not in direct contact with the elements.

Yes, the warning signs were ignored by the man on watch, creating a far more precarious situation. He only stepped out of sight of the hawser for a few seconds! As he did, the bow of the front fishing vessel we were towing dipped below the waves, placing a high level of stress on the front section of the towing line.

The explosion sounded like the blast from a battleship. A second explosion came when the snapped hawser came back. It obliterated the watchman's chair and ripped the quarter-inch steel door off of the aft hawser locker.

The entire ship came alive! They feared that the remnants of the hawser had killed the watchman or wrapped around the propellers of our ship.

It took the crew a good two hours to reestablish the tow, but it took far more than a cup of coffee to calm that poor sailor who had been on watch. Had he not chosen that particular moment to go into the locker, he would've been ripped in half by the returning hawser.

Upon evaluation it was determined that we had exceeded the safe limits of the tow at about twelve knots. Had we been more aware of the potential danger, that near-death situation could have been avoided.

God has given us all the warning signs we need to know that the end of time is near. Are we making the necessary preparations to deal with what is yet to come? Or are we spending too much time worrying about what might happen and not enough on what is right in front of us?

> *The explosion sounded like the blast from a battleship.*

The towline on this world is about to snap. We have been commissioned to spread the alarm. However, instead of spreading that alarm, we seem to be spending our time measuring the cord to determine exactly when it is going to break; all the time *knowing* that it will break.

Let's return to our mission to spread the alarm rather than continuing to measure the cord.

CHAPTER 21: SPIDERS!

Now therefore, fear the Lord, serve Him in sincerity and in truth, and put away the gods which your fathers served on the other side of the River and in Egypt. Serve the Lord! And if it seems evil to you to serve the Lord, choose for yourself this day whom you will serve, whether the gods which your fathers served that *were* on the other side of the River, or the gods of the Amorites, in whose land you dwell. But as for me and my house, we will serve the Lord. (Josh. 24:14, 15)

One of my main duties at Eaton's Neck Coast Guard Station was the repair and maintenance of the computer system that controlled the automated lighthouses throughout Long Island Sound. And on this day, one particular lighthouse off of Blackrock Harbor in Connecticut had lost the use of its radio telemetry device and gone into failsafe.

Each lighthouse on the Sound had a device that measured the density of the atmosphere. When there was sufficient fog density to warn ships, this device would automatically turn the foghorn on.

Incidentally, the foghorn at each lighthouse had its own unique sequence of tones. It is difficult to sense direction in the fog, but by hearing more than one horn, it becomes possible to get a rough idea of your location. For many people, a foghorn is just another noise near the water. But to those who navigated using those sounds on a regular basis, the distinction between horns was enough to let them know where they were.

In addition to the foghorn there was the light itself. Finally, some locations also included the control of a radio beacon (like the one near Blackrock Harbor did).

All of these variables could normally be controlled from the main console at Eaton's Neck Long Island. If there was a breakdown in the telemetry signal between Eaton's Neck and the remote site, however, then the remote site would go into a failsafe mode. Failsafe mode meant both the light and the foghorn turned on until the problem was corrected.

I was not looking forward to this particular trip, because someone had not used wise judgment in the placement of the foghorn. There was a deck about twenty feet above the water that went all the way around the base of the lighthouse and extended outward about four feet from the lighthouse itself. A tube that was about ten feet tall passed through the platform. To access the lighthouse, our boat needed to pull up to the lighthouse's base. From there the technician could jump to the ladder and scale the outside of the lighthouse, first going through the tube. The problem was that somebody had mounted the foghorn right at the top of that tube!

Once you jumped from the small boat to the ladder, the boat needed to pull back to keep from being smashed into the rocks. There was no beach; no place to go except up. With the foghorn going off every thirty seconds, you had to make your decision and maneuver fast (while carrying all your gear) to avoid being in the tube at the time of the next blast. If by chance you *were* in the tube when the foghorn went off, you would undoubtedly not hear anything for about a week! Ah! Now there's the rub.

Chapter 21: Spiders!

I had a small bag of tools and equipment with me when I made the trip to the stricken lighthouse. After surveying the situation, I told the coxswain to ease as close as he could to the ladder and then move forward just as the horn went off. This would give me maximum transit time (and eliminate the problem of not hearing anything for a week).

Everything seemed to go according to plan. The sky was blue and the seas were calm; conditions were ideal. As the coxswain moved forward, I stood on the bow, ready to jump. As soon as the horn went off, I leapt to the ladder and the coxswain pulled away. I started to climb. Then I made the mistake of looking up!

Now I have climbed many things, and I generally climb while looking down, because by looking down I can get a better bearing on my location. Here, though, I was about to enter a tube that was not much wider than I was (it would probably be difficult for me to fit comfortably in that tube today, but at that time in my life I was about forty pounds lighter, so it should not have been an issue). And when I looked up, I beheld, to my horror, the worst thing that I could have seen: spider webs!

I don't mind snakes, and I can deal with almost any other type of creature; however, I have always had a hard time with spiders. It appears I transmitted this to my daughters, for one of them once told me that she was the Al Capone of the spider world: she wanted the spider dead, she wanted the spider's family dead, and she wanted the house that the spider lived in burned to the ground!

I can relate to her. I remember many times as a youngster running through cornfields only to pick up one of those lovely, black-and-gold garden spiders. I can also remember our home in Fairhaven that had bushes directly in front of the back door; in just a few hours one of those lovely garden spiders could weave a web across those bushes. The bite of one of those fellows was similar to a bee sting, and that was not something that I looked forward to.

As I looked up at those spider webs in the tube, I did the thing that would be my downfall: I hesitated.

My mind weighed the possibilities. There was no way to go back, as the boat had already pulled away. Besides, I was inside the beginning of the tube, so I couldn't even signal the driver to turn around. And I realized that I was bigger than any of those little spiders; they were not black widow or brown recluse spiders, just harmless little insects. *Oh, excuse me!* I thought, *I guess they are not even actually insects!*

After this brief time of hesitation, I realized the other issue: the foghorn did not care whether I feared spiders or not! There really was only one option, and that was to go forward.

As my mind tried to get my feet to react to the new decision to move forward, they slowly began climbing higher. I was about one foot from the top of the tube when my ears and brain were shattered by the long horn blast!

I scrambled up the rest of the way to the deck, brushed off any traces of the web, and moved to the far side of the lighthouse, where there was a door to access the inside. I serviced the lighthouse while my ears rang … and they continued to do so for several days!

I used to wonder why they would try so hard to get people to make a decision during evangelistic series events. While taking part in one, the evangelist told me that if the window of opportunity passes and a decision has not been made, it becomes harder and harder for any person to make the necessary choice. Hesitation is one of our downfalls.

I have since witnessed this over and over, as I've seen people's resolve waver and fail. Theirs is not usually an instantaneous failure like mine was on that ladder, but nevertheless, if we do not choose promptly, quite often the desire to choose weakens.

You may have seen this in your own life regarding things that needed to be done … and that were never acted on. Life has a way of diminishing urgency. However, we are at a point in Earth's history where there is little time left to let opportunity slip by.

If you have heard the truth of Jesus Christ and are waiting to decide whether to accept Him or to continue on your own way, be aware that many situations can come between you and the decision for Jesus. The devil will use every opportunity to prevent this, which is the only *real* choice that we have.

I say *real* choice because *no* choice is, in fact, a choice. As I stood there on the ladder and did not choose to move forward or backward, I was making a choice.

God is holding out His hand. He is knocking at the door, and we have but to let Him in. There is no need to change your life. There is no need to correct the situations that we see around us. Only accept, and He will change our lives for us. Remember Joshua 24:15b: "As for me and my house, we will serve the Lord."

CHAPTER 22: THE TOWER

> And as Moses lifted up the serpent in the wilderness, even so must the Son of Man be lifted up, that whoever believes in Him should not perish but have eternal life. For God so loved the world that He gave His only begotten Son, that whoever believes in Him should not perish but have everlasting life. (John 3:14-16)

John 3:16 is perhaps the best-known verse in the entire New Testament. However, many of those who have memorized it are unfamiliar with verses 14 and 15. I find it hard to separate the three. In fact, the entire story of Nicodemus is one of the most important stories in the New Testament. It is easy to see why it is believed to be the focal point of the Gospel.

The reference in the quoted verses is, of course, to the brazen serpent in the wilderness and to how the children of Israel could, by just looking at the brazen serpent, escape being hurt by the other serpents' attack.

I always found it interesting that looking at the serpent did not eliminate the snakes. Nor was there a guarantee that the Israelites would not be bitten. The only guarantee offered was that they would survive; and so it is with us.

Chapter 22: The Tower

Accepting Jesus Christ is no guarantee that the old serpent, the devil, will not still cause us grief and problems. The guarantee is that Christ has won, and we will, in the end, go home with Him.

Once a year at that station in Alaska, the lights on top of the radio tower needed to be changed. Of course if one failed, it would have to be changed right then, but the lights normally lasted well past one year. However, even if the lights were still working, it was important to change them before they failed.

The station radio signal was not supposed to be off the air more than three seconds in thirty days. This was usually the amount of time it took to transfer power from one transmitter and generator to the complete backup system.

There was a huge switch that was thrown to disconnect one transmitter and engage the other. The one-and-a-half million watts of energy caused a tremendous arc when the switch was activated. This transfer was done live. The three-second switch over was usually not enough to even be noticed by those who used the navigational signal (it was, of course, registered in our station records).

So if you couldn't be off the air more than three seconds, how did you change a light bulb 2,000 feet straight up? The only way was to climb the tower while it was energized!

Why they chose January as the time to change the light, I will never understand. But once it was done the first time, it became the date forever after to make the change.

There were no volunteers to climb a tower 2,000 feet high in the sort of temperatures that we experienced in January. Meanwhile I had done a lot of work on the mast of a ship over the years and had climbed many towers. Heights never seemed to bother me, though I was sympathetic to those who had trouble with the concept. So rather than make somebody do something that they were scared to attempt, I decided to climb the tower myself.

I faced two challenges. First, there was a track that ran along the tower after you reached its narrow point about fifty feet up. Ideally you could attach a sliding belt there for safety. It *sounds* like a good idea. However,

The radio tower at Cape Sarichef. It had electrifying views!

several years of weather had made that track less slippery than it was meant to be, and for all practical purposes useless. The other issue was that you did not want to be in contact with the ground and the tower at the same time, as one-and-a-half million watts of energy would fry you fairly quickly (for some reason, I was not into the smell of frying flesh)!

We set up signals so that the transmitter could be taken offline for a few seconds. I would jump on the tower, climb up two steps, then the transmitter would be reenergized and retuned with me as a part of the antenna. I had a bag with several replacement light bulbs (just in case) and my camera. I wore government-issue combat boots with a good, solid steel shank in the arch, a good pair of gloves, and foul weather gear. This all was done on the last day of December so that the time required for getting me *off* of the tower would be in *January*; and thus we would not exceed our three seconds a month.

Standing at the base of the tower, I waited for the signal to be given. It came. Up I went.

I did not feel any different being on an energized tower of one-and-a-half million watts, but I would always wonder if it had an effect on my overall health.

Chapter 22: The Tower

As I mentioned before, I normally like to climb by looking down, but in this case I wanted to focus on the tower rather than the ground. This was going to be a bit higher than I had climbed in the past (and would take a bit longer, since the safety track didn't work). I climbed for about ten minutes,

> One-and-a-half million watts of energy would fry you fairly quickly

stopped and strapped myself to the tower in order to rest for at least five minutes, then continued. I repeated this process for over two hours (I know there were others watching me from the ground the entire time that I was climbing, but I am not sure how that was supposed to be a comfort).

When I reached the top, the tower was moving four to five feet to the left and right. It was now narrow enough that I could put my arms completely around it. I tied myself to the tower so I could remove the light bulbs and replace them without falling off and down those 2,000 feet.

I did get some lovely pictures of the station and buildings from a third of a mile up, looking straight down. I sent copies to my wife.

She replied, *Who in the world took these pictures?*

There were times when a two-month delay in our letters made things a little easier.

Jesus tells us that if we jump from this world to Him and cling to Him, He will keep us safe. He is not guaranteeing that the wind and weather will not affect us, and He is not guaranteeing that holding onto Him will be easy. What He promises is that if we focus on Him, He will take care of the rest.

As difficult as the climb may be, He has a safety cord attached. The only way we can fall is to jump free.

Even when the tower of this world is swinging four feet to the left and four feet to the right, we can be secure in knowing that He has hold of us. Look straight ahead to Him. Do not try to look up, and do not try to look into the past, but focus on Jesus Christ … and you will be safe.

CHAPTER 23: MUTTLEY

For whom the Lord loves He chastens, and scourges every son whom He receives. (Heb. 12:6)

God sends trials not only to test us but to hone us; to sharpen us for what is to come. Sometimes it feels like God is hitting me with a two by four to get my attention … and I still don't listen. It is only when we listen to Him that we truly begin to avoid unnecessary chastening.

There are times when animals can help us understand what we as people need to do. A few sheep stories will be coming up (I find that sheep and people have a lot in common) but this story is about a dog: our station mascot in Alaska, Muttley.

Muttley was an Alaskan Malamute Husky cross, and he could never stay inside very long. He enjoyed the cold. He enjoyed the snow. He enjoyed just being outside! Even in extreme temperatures, he would huddle next to a building, tuck his nose between his legs, and snooze.

Chapter 23: Muttley

On one particular day (and I use the term loosely, because there was no sun at that time of year, just eternal night), Muttley was snoozing near the corner of the building where we had our recreation area. We could watch him through the windows, but we wished he would learn to stay inside. However, if we brought him in, within minutes he'd want to go back out (remembering this today, Muttley reminds me of the two Australian Shepherds that I currently have: they are always on the wrong side of the door).

This was one of those lovely winter days where the wind was not only cold but strong enough to sweep you off your feet. If you wanted to go from one building to another, you had to do it hand over hand on guide ropes. If you didn't *have* hands to hold onto the rope, it could be even more dangerous. For example, the island had funny little puffins. These were plump little birds, and when the wind blew as strongly as it did that day, they often were seen bouncing down the road!

There was nothing Muttley enjoyed better than chasing puffins, so when a couple of them went bouncing by, it caught Muttley's attention. His head flipped up, his body tensed, and he took off like a rocket, chasing the birds.

As soon as he cleared the corner of the building, the wind carried Muttley off just as it had carried the birds! He went bouncing head over heels down the road.

We had seen this many times before. We knew that sooner or later, Muttley would regain his footing and crawl back. This day was no exception. About fifteen minutes passed, then we saw Muttley crawling close to the ground until he was in the lee of the building. Once he was out of the wind he settled down, tucked his nose back between his legs, and relaxed.

Less than five minutes later, two more puffins went bouncing by. Muttley's head perked up again, his body tensed, and he took off like a rocket. Once again, as soon as he cleared the lee of the building, Muttley was picked up from behind, flipped head over heels, and bounced down the road just like the puffins. And ten to fifteen minutes later, Muttley was crawling back on his belly until he was in the lee of the building where he could once again relax.

That is, until a few minutes later, when another puffin would go bouncing by and—you guessed it!—Muttley repeated the cycle.

This went on with what seemed to be an infinite number of puffins. I don't think Muttley ever learned his lesson. The excitement of the chase always exceeded the risk.

All too often, God tries to correct our action with that telltale two by four upside the head, and all too often, the excitement of the action He's trying to correct is too great for us to give up. Yet Jesus tells us, "He who has begun a good work in us will complete *it* until the day of Jesus Christ. (Phil. 1:6b).

There will come a time in your life, as it is coming in mine, when Jesus will need to use fewer and fewer corrections with us. This happens as we draw closer and closer to Him.

The way we draw closer to Jesus is to spend more time in His Word and strengthen that relationship with Him. It is, in fact, all about relationship.

CHAPTER 24: MISSIONARY'S FAITH

Behold the proud, his soul is not upright in him; but the just shall live by his faith. (Hab. 2:4)

I have always loved stories of faith. We are all saved by the righteousness of Jesus Christ, and it is His faith that directs our steps.

I have also always been amazed how little faith I seem to have in comparison to some that I have met, such as Simus Kudirka.

This story takes place after I was discharged from the Coast Guard and while I was working as an engineer in Massachusetts. It is about one of my two by four experiences.

Two of my responsibilities in my engineering job were troubleshooting and lecturing worldwide. On this occasion I had been in Tokyo for several weeks lecturing on plasma physics, and I was now scheduled to return to the States.

I have been very fortunate and at the same time unfortunate. Fortunate in that I've had the opportunity to travel the world, and I mean that literally. You could drop me blindfolded in any one of twenty major cities from China to Germany, Japan to Ireland, and I would know where I was within minutes. I also say unfortunate in that this resulted in my being away from home so much that I accumulated four-and-a-half million air miles.

With success always come sacrifice. In retrospect, I would have preferred less success and more time with my family. On this trip, it had been nearly a month since I had been home. I was not only tired of eating with sticks, I missed my family terribly.

An emergency arose in Osaka prior to my return, so I made a side trip there, corrected the situation, and then tried to make my connection in Tokyo to return to the United States. However, because of a rail accident, my bullet train to Tokyo was delayed. As a result I missed my flight home.

By this time in my life I spent much time on my knees. I had come to realize that God could, and would, perform miracles. I had witnessed and been a part of many such miracles. What I had not yet learned quite as well as I should have was the art of listening!

I prayed and asked God to help me get home to my family (the travel agent had told me I was stuck in Tokyo for several weeks). As soon as I got off my knees, the phone rang.

It was the travel agent. He was excited and told me that he could get me a flight in three days from Tokyo to Hawaii, then from Hawaii to San Francisco, and after an overnight in San Francisco, on to Boston. The total time of all these connections meant that I would be home in about six days.

It should've occurred to me that the call came immediately after my prayer. Now, I'm not saying that I'm stubborn … I'm shouting it!

Many times I had made flight arrangements that were better than my company travel agent, so I told him to just never mind; I would make my own connection.

There are no coincidences in this world. Everything that happens has a reason for happening.

Over the next thirty minutes, I managed to get a flight the next day from Tokyo to Guam, then from Guam to Hawaii, from Hawaii to

Chapter 24: Missionary's Faith

San Francisco, and finally from San Francisco to Boston. The difference from the agent's offer was that my connections would get me home three days earlier! I booked the flights and packed my bags.

The flight to Guam was through a Chinese airline, on an old DC-3 that was probably built during the Korean War! The DC-3 aircraft is an old propeller-driven plane. It was worse than any amusement ride you could imagine. Plus, these were the days before tobacco-free flights, and everyone on the plane except me was smoking. The man next to me was also carrying his chickens on his lap, and the turbulence set the chickens free a dozen times! I don't think I have ever been on a worse flight in my life.

When we reached Guam, we had to circle the airport because we were so late in arriving. As we waited for another plane to take off, I realized it was my connecting flight to Hawaii. When we finally got into the terminal, I ran to the ticket desk to find out when the next flight was to Hawaii. It appeared that the airport in Guam was not as busy as I would have liked it to be, as I discovered that there would not be another flight for two days! The upside of it all was that I got to see the island of Guam inside and out.

When I finally made my connection to Hawaii, I realized that I was going to be boarding the exact same flight that I would've been on had I listen to the travel agent in the first place. The only difference now was that instead of being in first class, I was in the cheap seats; something that I was not used to.

There's something about that extra three or four inches in seat size and the ability to recline it into a bed that makes long trips just a little bit more enjoyable. I guess you could say that I had been spoiled by all that travel, because in most cases I would get automatically bumped to first class. On this occasion, though, first class was full. So there I was, sitting next to a small four-year-old boy and his mother. I at least had the aisle seat, while his mother sat by the window.

It turned out that this four-year-old boy was the male equivalent of my daughter. That is, he was not only sociable but extremely talkative. I found it quite entertaining and enjoyed listening to his stories. A good storyteller loves to hear a good story!

It appeared that his parents were missionaries in the Philippines, and his father was translating the Bible into one of the many dialects there. But his grandmother was ill, so the church (some small Baptist church in Massachusetts) had raised money to pay for him and his mother to fly home.

The story was touching, and the boy was adorable. After a while I turned to his mother and told her just how adorable he was, then I asked if they were continuing on directly to Boston. She told me that they had to stay overnight in San Francisco and then catch a flight in the morning. I let her know that I was on the same connecting flight. When we compared tickets, we found that we were sitting together on that flight as well.

I asked her where she was staying in San Francisco. She matter-of-factly told me that she had no idea. She did not have so much as a nickel of cash and no way to pay for a room! I asked her what she was planning to do, then. She repeated that she had no idea but that God would provide.

Their trip to the mission field had been paid by God, their accommodations in the mission field had been covered by God, and this trip had been ordained by God, she said. She was sure that God would take care of any arrangements necessary. She was not apprehensive, she was not nervous; she was just sure that God was in charge.

It is one thing to be sure that God is in charge when you're alone, but when you have a four-year-old child and no way of being sure that you will not be sleeping on a bench in the airport? That's more faith than I'm used to.

I knew that I had a company-paid room waiting for me in San Francisco. I asked her if she would be interested in using it while I sought out a relative who lived in San Jose just about an hour from the airport. I told her that they could order whatever they wanted from room service, and to do the same for breakfast. I would cover all of her expenses.

When we arrived in San Francisco, I took her to the hotel and told the maître d' what I had told her. After making all the payment arrangements, I collected my rental car and drove to my uncle's house in San Jose.

Rising at 4 a.m., I drove back to the hotel and picked up the young missionary and her son. On the ride to the airport, she smiled, touched my hand, and said, "See, I told you God would take care of everything. He just needed you to do the work for Him."

In Boston we said our goodbyes. I wept as I realized that I had been meant to be on that flight ... but God had first needed to move me from first class to coach to accomplish His miracle for somebody else.

That young missionary touched my heart. She reminded me that we can put all of our trust, all of our steps in Jesus's hand.

It is not always about us, but God can use us in the greater picture.

CHAPTER 25: ENGINEER JOHN

Trust in the Lord with all your heart, and lean not on your own understanding; in all your ways acknowledge Him, and He shall direct your paths. (Prov. 3:5, 6)

This next story is another one of those long stories, so I might as well start at the beginning. I had been working as a microwave engineer in a small company in Massachusetts, and it seemed like every project that I worked on was turned into a weapon of some sort.

One project that I was particularly excited about was connected to the space shuttle program. I felt there was no way that *that* could be used as a weapon. Then this turned out to be the ill-fated space shuttle that exploded, and I realized that maybe I needed to switch from design engineering to something more passive.

Chapter 25: Engineer John

I took a job with another company in Massachusetts. This one was involved in plasma processing equipment (plasma is the fourth state of matter and is used in the design of semiconductors). My job was initially to train and manage the field service personnel. After six months I was made the director of customer service.

While working for this company, I was just finishing my master's degree in business. I used the work that I was doing as a basis for my thesis: a business plan to make the company run more efficiently. Also right about this time, the company was experiencing a hostile takeover.

There are a limited number of things that a company can do to stop a hostile takeover. Though not the best choice, what this company did was to close the division that I was working in and write off the three million dollars in engineering expenses that had been spent that year. The administration gave layoff notices to numerous engineers and laborers. I would be secure because of my position in customer service; a group that would have to be maintained for at least seven years.

This would (in fact it did) drive the price of their stock up and, they hoped, make it difficult for the buying company to take over. However, the action did not stop the takeover.

The president of the new corporation sought out each department head to evaluate their purchase. When he came into my office, I explained to him that my division had been closed prematurely and that there was a lot of profit yet to be seen if it were managed correctly.

He looked at me and asked if I had anything to back up my words.

My business plan just happened to be sitting in front of me on my desk, so I handed it to him. I told the president that this was how I would run the division, and I could promise that it would be profitable within one year.

He smiled and gave me that look of, *yes, I've heard this before*. He left the room but took my paper with him.

I did not hear from him for several weeks, so I figured it was a lost cause. But then I received a phone call. The president of the corporation asked me if I thought that this would really work.

I answered without a doubt that it would.

He said he liked my confidence, but he would be watching. Then he was silent. After a minute or two of this uncomfortable silence, he told me that I was now the new director of the company, and he would expect me to keep him abreast of my progress.

When he hung up, I stood there in shock. I wasn't sure if what had just happened had really happened. Not only was I going to be given the chance to test my theories, it came with a substantial raise!

One of the problems which I needed to fix was a bad habit that the previous company had had of shipping equipment to meet the deadline whether it worked or not. They had expected the field service crew to get it working in the field.

Probably one of the reasons I wound up so successful in correcting these error situations for the new plasma company was prior experience I had gained working in the field service division of a company called Heathkit. The problems that we had seen there resulted from people who did not follow the directions. We wound up with the strangest problems imaginable … and it taught me a whole different way of troubleshooting, since I was not fixing things that worked but rather things that had never had a *chance* to work!

Another problem that I had to face in my new role at the plasma company was that most of the intelligence and senior engineers had already been laid off. I immediately set out to reverse several of these layoffs, but I was successful with just a few.

One such fellow had only had one year left until being vested in his retirement. He had been laid off so the old company could avoid paying his full retirement. He was a quiet man, and I had had the opportunity to work with him on occasion. This engineer, we will call him John, was a very good engineer, even if his social skills left a lot to be desired (he was quiet to a fault). I knew that if he stayed on for a year or two, he would pass the age when he could probably get hired into another company. But I also knew that he could retire in a few years fully vested in the company we were now in.

I called John into my office and explained to him what my intentions were for the company. We would be going into a totally different marketplace, which would require alterations to many of the products that we made for the semiconductor industry. I also told him that I had a lot of faith in his ability. Then I asked him if he would be willing to stay on and help me with this project.

Chapter 25: Engineer John

John thought about it for just a few minutes. Then he looked at me and gave one of his long speeches which consisted of one word: "Yes!"

The people whom I gathered to run this new company were not necessarily the "best" people available, but they were a crew that I could not have assembled better. If you treat people with the understanding that they work to live (not live to work), then you give them respect from the janitor to the chief engineer! When you treat them with the love that all people deserve, they will do anything for you. This must never be abused, but it can be used for the betterment of all. We started to turn things around.

One of the last pieces of equipment to be shipped from the old company had been a machine designed to etch the plate holes on circuit boards. (Plate holes allow connections to be made between multiple layers of a single circuit board. You could almost say that it is like a transistor, but on a circuit board level. The connections are then made by plating through those holes with gold, thus connecting up to fifteen layers of a circuit board.)

The machine in question had been sent to McDonnell Douglas in St. Louis, Missouri, but it was not fully tested before it was shipped. The field technicians had now spent nearly a month onsite and had been unable to get the machine operational.

One Monday I received a call from the president of McDonnell Douglas. He told me that they were shipping the entire device back, and they wanted reimbursement not only for shipping but for the equipment and loss of production.

We were looking at $600,000 for the equipment alone, not to mention all the extras! The total bill could have been the straw that broke the camel's back for our new company. I had to think quickly.

I told him that if he would give me until Friday, I would personally come and bring the design engineer with me. If we did not get the machine operating by Friday, I would meet all his demands, including the additional expenses. When I hung up, I realized that I had just placed this entire operation in the balance. Now I had to *move* quickly.

I soon discovered that the design engineer was John. This brought relief but also fear … because John did not fly. I felt confident that between John and me, we could get it running. The question was, could we do it in time?

If we had to waste twenty-four hours driving to St. Louis, we would only have one or two days to accomplish our goal. The only possible solution, in my view, was to fly first thing in the morning and be there by 11 a.m. Tuesday, which would give us an extra two days to accomplish the task.

I called John in and explained the situation. I asked him what parts he felt we might need to bring with us and if he would be willing to fly just this once. I saw John start to shake. For a second, I thought that maybe we didn't have a chance after all. He stopped and got hold of himself, then told me that he would fly with me in the morning.

Trying to make the situation as comfortable as possible for John, I booked two business class tickets out of Boston at 6 a.m. I told him I would pick him up at his house in time to make the flight. He sat for the entire drive to Boston without saying a single word, clutching his briefcase to his chest. In the meantime I was praying that it would be a smooth flight. At the airport, as we approached the plane, I saw John once again begin to shake.

People who have a fear of flying should never be condemned. This is a real fear: it can be the most horrifying experience someone will ever face. I knew that day that I had to help John through it.

I comforted him with the words that I had literally hundreds of hours of flying and that I would be there to help him. As the plane took off from Logan Airport, I saw John's knuckles turn white on the edge of his seat. I reached over and put my hand on his. I kept saying quietly, "It is okay, John. It is okay." When his tears started to come, I again tried to soothe him.

Then John turned to me and told me he had to tell me a story.

He told me of a young engineer, right out of school during World War II, who was also a pilot. After he had graduated, this man had been taken into the Army Air Corps and had spent several years dropping bombs over Europe. He had never missed his target nor had he lost an aircraft.

Near the end of the war, he had realized that his missions were no longer military targets; they were civilian. The killing was taking its toll; the young man was having a hard time dealing with the deaths of innocent people.

Chapter 25: Engineer John

He went to command and told them that he could not go on. Today we would understand that he was suffering from PTSD. His emotional stability must soon collapse.

Because of his record, they decided to ship the man back to the United States and let him become an instructor. After all, the war in Europe was winding down, and soon the Pacific would be the only front. The man realized he did not have an option, but he felt that being an instructor was better than being the one dropping the bombs.

After quite some time, command approached him again and told him that if he would do one more mission, they would let him retire from the service. He was told that he could pick his own crew and that he would train with two other crews for this final mission.

He agreed to the conditions and began the training. One of his friends wound up in one of the other crews. They would fly from Arizona to Boston, pretend to drop their load, then bank up and away from the blast as hard and fast as they could. The nature of the training told them that whatever they were going to drop was big, but they had no idea of what was to come.

> *John reached into his bag and pulled out a photo album. He said, "These are off the record."*

When the day of the mission finally came, the three crews were called together to draw straws. They were told that because of their hard banking to leave the area, their own bomb sites would be ineffective in determining the damage. The short straw would fly the first mission. The middle straw would follow behind about two hours later and take pictures of the drop site. They reconciled themselves to their instructions.

His friend drew the short straw: the crew of the Enola Gay would drop the bomb.

At this point in the story, John reached into his bag and pulled out a photo album. He said, "These are off the record." They were copies of what he had seen two hours after the bomb was dropped. With tears in his eyes, John showed me the bomb site pictures of ground zero from both Hiroshima and Nagasaki.

With a trembling voice, John told me that for forty years, he had not slept without nightmares of 100,000 people being vaporized in an instant. I wept with him. "Since I retired," he said, "I have never been in a plane until this day." He also told me that he would probably take all of this to his grave.

As we wept, I told him about how one man gave His life for all of mankind and bore on His shoulders the burden for everyone who ever lived and ever will live. I told him how He died of a broken heart; and not from the cross. How He bore this alone, and how when He cried out, "My God, My God, Why have You forsaken Me?" He was utterly and completely alone.

Continuing, I told him how Jesus wanted to take even this burden from John.

We held hands and prayed. John gave his life to the Lord that day. Though I do not know if it removed all of those dreams from his night visions, I do know that he changed.

We went on to St. Louis and completed our task by Thursday. We got the equipment up and running, and McDonnell Douglas was back in production.

A bond grew between John and I for the rest of his time with that small company. In that first year, we turned that $3 million loss into a profit of $100,000. John would retire two years later, but with his help and that of every member of my crew, we remained profitable until I left the company some six years later.

We all have our nightmares and our fears, but Jesus is there to wipe away every tear if we but ask Him into our lives.

Jesus promises us peace beyond understanding. If He can do it for John after what he experienced, then He can do it for all of us.

CHAPTER 26: ANECHOIC CHAMBER

And at the ninth hour Jesus cried out with a loud voice, saying, "Eloi, Eloi, lama sabachthani?" which is translated, "My God, My God, why have You forsaken Me?" (Mark 15:34)

It is said that when one loses one of their senses, the other senses pick up the slack. I'm not sure if this is really true, although I know that one of the cruelest (but totally effective) means of torture is total sensory deprivation.

I do wonder, however: what would you do if you lost *all* of your senses?

While working as a radio frequency design engineer, I often conducted tests in what is called an anechoic chamber. This is a specially designed chamber that looks like a pyramid placed on its side. In the apex of the pyramid we would place an antenna, and we suspended a transmitter near the base. We then rotated the transmitter and measured the emissions from the device. This allowed us to determine if there was any leakage or spurious emissions and then make the necessary corrections.

The chamber was constructed to absorb all energy except what was directed at the antenna. This included light and sound. Additionally, the chamber was large enough to suspend a person. If you were to put someone in a harness, secure their hands and feet, and suspend them in the chamber, their senses of sight, sound, and touch would be removed.

I have always been curious by nature, so I asked to be suspended for five minutes, just to feel what it would be like to be devoid of all senses but smell.

Once the door was closed, I experienced total darkness. This was the first real shock, because I don't mean it was just dark … there was absolutely *no light* of any type. Try closing your eyes right now: you will still see some light through your eyelids. Now, while they are still closed, cover your eyes with your hands; you can *begin* to understand what total darkness is like.

Removing sound for yourself is a little more difficult. Even when you have severe hearing loss, often there is still some sound. But not in the chamber. You can speak, but you can only hear through your own bone structure.

And finally, as I said, if suspended with your hands and your feet secured, your sense of touch is greatly restricted.

So there I was: my eyes wide open but I saw nothing, my ears uncovered but I heard nothing, and I could touch nothing. Put all this together and I started to feel strange after about one minute.

By the time two minutes had gone by, I was feeling very uneasy.

Between two and three minutes, I started to hear a faint pounding sound: it turned out to be my own heartbeat.

When they finally opened the door after five minutes, I realized just how intense sensory deprivation must be. To endure that for several hours, not knowing if you would ever see anyone who you loved again? It must be horrific.

Chapter 26: Anechoic Chamber

I would like to share with you a quotation from one of my favorite authors:

> Satan with his fierce temptations wrung the heart of Jesus. The Saviour could not see through the portals of the tomb. Hope did not present to Him His coming forth from the grave a conqueror, or tell Him of the Father's acceptance of the sacrifice. He feared that sin was so offensive to God that Their separation was to be eternal. Christ felt the anguish which the sinner will feel when mercy shall no longer plead for the guilty race. It was the sense of sin, bringing the Father's wrath upon Him as man's substitute, that made the cup He drank so bitter, and broke the heart of the Son of God. (White, *The Desire of Ages*, p. 753).

We were not designed to be isolated, solitary creatures. It was always the intention that we would be in a symbiotic relationship eternally with God.

When you're feeling alone and separated from anyone else, God is there. When you feel no one cares about you, God does. When you think you have no place to turn, you can turn to God.

We live in a society where loneliness has caused people to take their own lives. The truth of the matter is that we never need to be alone.

CHAPTER 27: THE SHEEP STORY

My sheep hear My voice, and I know them, and they follow Me. (John 10:27)

Stories are about everyday life. If we take the time to notice, they are all around us.

For example, my wife and I have had sheep for over twenty-five years, and for us it is easy to understand why Jesus uses sheep so often in His illustrations.

I remember one time I visited a family who was reading a set of Bible story books. The mother pulled me to one side and told me that she was having a problem with one of the stories (I think she told me this knowing that I had been a shepherd for many years, and was seeking my input). The story told of how the shepherd sheared his sheep, and afterward the lambs no longer could figure out who their mothers were.

Chapter 27: The Sheep Story

She could not fathom how a lamb would not know its own mother, so she had removed the story from the book. When she showed it to me, the story was heavily redacted.

I smiled and told her a little story of my own. At one time my wife and I had a flock of about thirty-five sheep, twenty of which were lambs. The time came to shear the mothers.

We separated the lambs and brought the mothers out (the lambs themselves were too young to shear, so it was only the ewes getting a haircut). This was before we were shearing for ourselves, so we had a professional come to do the job. After she was done shearing, we put the mothers back with the rest of the flock.

We were surprised to see the total chaos that ensued. Each lamb would go to the wrong ewe and try to nurse, only to be booted away. It appeared that they couldn't recognize their mothers by either sight or smell! Normally the lambs relied on scent, but between the absence of all of their wool and the odor of the shearing grease (which would take at least twenty-four hours to wash off), all the mothers smelled different. After a few minutes of this confusion, the ewes went on the offensive and sought out their own lambs.

I then told the mother, "So you see, the story is correct."

This illustration soon became "The Sheep Story," and I used it before my next sermon. Of course I removed all indications of who I was talking about, but I could see that mother slouching down in her seat, much to the enjoyment of her kids! I then went on to tell a different sheep story every week for the next three months.

There are many stories every shepherd can share. For instance, if I were to walk in the field and yell, "Hey, babies!" there would be a stampede of sheep gathering around me. Why is it that my sheep flock to me when I call them? It is because the sheep and I have a relationship; they know me and know my voice.

We are Jesus's sheep, and He calls us by name. His own know His voice, and they respond. Revelation 3:20 says, "Behold, I stand at the door and knock. If anyone hears My voice and opens the door, I will come in to him and dine with him, and he with Me."

We cannot expect to hear Jesus's voice if we don't have a relationship with Him. The only way to develop that relationship is to spend time in His Word. If we spend time in His Word, we will hear His voice.

CHAPTER 28: WHOOPI AND THE SWAMP

What do you think? If a man has a hundred sheep, and one of them goes astray, does he not leave the ninety-nine and go to the mountains to seek the one that is straying? And if he should find it, assuredly, I say to you, he rejoices more over that *sheep* than over the ninety-nine that did not go astray. Even so it is not the will of your Father who is in heaven that one of these little ones should perish. (Matt. 18:12-14)

Over the years we have had many sheep, but there is always one that especially comes to mind, and that is Whoopi. Whoopi was one-of-a-kind! There seemed to be no fence that she couldn't find the weak point of and escape, and no trouble that she might get into that she did not find.

Jim was a handyman and could do most anything, but needed a place to stay. So for room and board plus wages, he spent several weeks with us helping to paint our house.

Jim also enjoyed animals and was eager to help me with the sheep. We did not have a lot at this time; only about seven, as each year we sold the lambs and kept the mothers. Still, I knew each one by name, and they all knew me. (These were not registered sheep, but they were a Lincoln and Finn crossbreed. They were not only large but had excellent quality wool. Since my wife and I were both spinners, this quality was of primary concern.)

One evening, as always, I called the sheep back to the barn to close them in for the night. Bringing the sheep in at night was for their own safety and our peace of mind: there were many predators when you lived in what my coworkers called "the boonies." I counted heads as they entered the barn and discovered there was one missing: Whoopi.

> I started to become concerned. In the past when I had looked for Whoopi and called her name, she would come.

Now this was not the first time that Whoopi had come up missing, so Jim and I immediately checked the nearest neighbor's garden. But we found no Whoopi. We then went down our isolated road in the other direction, but still found no Whoopi. At this point in time, I started to become concerned. In the past when I had looked for Whoopi and called her name, she would come. This time there was no sign of her.

We returned to our starting point and were trying to decide our next move when, in the distance, we heard a faint and muffled, "Baa!" This was before my hearing loss, so I could sense the direction by listening to the sound. It appeared to be coming from our swamp!

This was a marshy area that never seemed to freeze, even in the winter. Because of the danger it presented, we had fenced it off from the pasture. But the closer Jim and I got to the fenced area, the louder Whoopi's cry became.

Following the fence, we found an area where the bottom had been lifted and an escape had occurred. Some twenty feet into the swamp, we could see Whoopi's head just above the surface.

Chapter 28: Whoopi and the Swamp

Now let me explain: Whoopi was fairly large and weighed over 150 pounds. This meant that the majority of her body weight was buried in mud. The more she struggled, the deeper she would go. We had to figure out a way to get her out as soon as possible.

For the house painting, Jim had been using staging along the side of the house which consisted of two by eight boards. We decided that it might be possible to place these boards on the surface of the swamp and work our way out to Whoopi.

It took several boards to reach her. I wasn't sure how she had gotten this far in. She kept moving and gradually sinking.

Doesn't it seem like this is how we all get ourselves into so much trouble? We start to sink, but instead of turning from the evil, we continue on until we find ourselves trapped; then we can't return or even move!

When we finally reached Whoopi's location, we were faced with a new problem: how to extract a 150-pound sheep from the mud.

Have you ever tried to pull something out of the mud? Maybe you have stepped in mud with boots on, only to have the boot pulled off your foot as you try to step out. There are times when it seems like the little force it took to step into something is multiplied tenfold when you try to step out. And so it is with sin: we find ourselves without the ability to escape.

As I mentioned in a previous story, one of the most horrible things I was taught when I was little was the idea that when we go into places where we should not be, our guardian angel leaves us to our own devices and waits outside. There can be nothing farther from the truth! Jesus has told us that He will never leave us nor forsake us.

Kneeling in front of Whoopi at the end of those planks, I offered a prayer. Then, reaching down, I grabbed hold of the wool on her back and pulled.

I am not a weak man, but I am not Hercules. I didn't think I would be able to overcome the suction of the mud. However, as I was pulling, I rose from a kneeling position to my feet, pulling Whoopi back onto the boards.

As soon as I got her up, I grabbed her around the middle and carried her backwards to safety. When I reached the fence, I lowered her over it and watched her try to shake the mud off her body. That was something neither one of us would be able to do without a good washdown! By the time I caught up to Whoopi with the hose, she was at the door to the barn waiting to get in. She wanted to have this experience over.

Still, Whoopi was happy. And I was happy too, even though I knew this would not be the last time she would escape.

I know that the day I pulled Whoopi from the swamp, there was an angel pulling along with me! Sometimes it seems like there's no end to the amount of trouble that Jesus redeems us from. Yet there is no point when He tells us, "That's it! I'm done with you." Isn't it wonderful to have such a Savior?!

CHAPTER 29: EMMA AND THE BEAR

Be sober, be vigilant; because your adversary the devil walks about like a roaring lion, seeking whom he may devour. (1 Peter 5:8)

nimals may not have our level of intelligence, but God has given all creatures instincts and the ability to love.

While Emma, my youngest daughter, was growing up, one of her chores was supposed to be caring for the animals (I say "supposed to be" because, like any teenager, life got in the way and not all the chores were done without protest). One evening as Emma went down to call the sheep into the barn, she noticed that all the ewes were huddled near it, close to the fence that blocked the way to the swamp. Their heads were together and their rears facing outward. Meanwhile the ram was circling the ewes and pawing at the ground.

Something was amiss. My daughter didn't know what the problem was, so she started to walk into the field. As she moved in that direction, her pony Peanut grabbed her shirt from behind and pulled her back.

Peanut stood 14.2 hands tall, putting him height-wise right at the border between pony and horse. He came from a riding farm and was along in years, but despite his age, he had developed a tight bond with Emma. My daughter immediately turned around and tried to chastise Peanut, but he walked around in front of her; and every time she started to move forward, he bared his teeth.

Peanut loved Emma and had never acted this way before. She did not know how to respond to his actions, so she immediately came up to the house to tell me what was going on. Together we went back down to the barn to try to figure out what was happening. I saw the sheep and the ram doing their thing off to the side, and Peanut seemed to be comfortable with my presence.

As we stood there, we saw the tall bamboo on the other side of the fence moving. Then we heard a low grunting sound. I quickly called the sheep into the barn along with Peanut and closed the doors.

Beyond that fence, the area opened up to the woods and the pond that was adjacent to our property. Because of our many fences and the presence of the sheep, we had not had problems with bears in the past; but I now let Emma know that there was quite probably just that on the other side of that fence. The sheep had been huddling for protection with the ram standing guard, and Peanut must have also sensed the danger. He had been trying to protect Emma from the bear's presence.

The devil is always trying to find a way to attack and devour. He knows better than anybody that the end is near, but he still seeks to devour as many souls as he can before Christ's return.

The Bible, on the other hand, tells us, "Therefore submit to God. Resist the devil and he will flee from you. Draw near to God and He will draw near to you" (James 4:7, 8a). The true meaning of this text is the message that the way to resist the devil is to submit to God. He, meaning Jesus, will cause the devil to flee from us.

There are many dangers in this world of evil, and you do not have the power to protect yourself from these forces. Our only sure protection is a relationship with Jesus Christ.

CHAPTER 30: LOST WITHOUT KNOWLEDGE

All Scripture *is* given by inspiration of God, and *is* profitable for doctrine, for reproof, for correction, for instruction in righteousness, that the man of God may be complete, thoroughly equipped for every good work. (2 Tim. 3:16, 17)

It has been said that the Bible is the number one bestselling book in the world, and that at the same time it is probably the least read. Earlier I mentioned how at one time I worked as a consultant for Heathkit. This was a company that manufactured kits for all kinds of equipment. It was always interesting to see who followed directions and who did their own thing. By not following directions, a kit could easily result in a collection of errors. Not following the Bible's directions in life can create even greater problems.

I have always tried to make it a habit to read the instructions. Now, that's no guarantee that I'll understand what I'm reading, but at least I'll have something to recall from memory (even a computer can't help you if the information has never been entered!).

Chapter 30: Lost Without Knowledge

It is not hard to see that people who are not used to following directions (or at least inquiring as to how things work) may face more issues than the rest of us.

It was a beautiful day in my Active days near the edge of Georges Bank, the drop-off point for the continental shelf located a few hundred miles due east of Boston. It was one of those days when the ocean was as calm as glass and you could see all the way to the horizon. The sun was just beginning to set, and the beautiful red skies reminded me of that old saying, "Red sky at night, sailors' delight. Red sky at morning, sailors take warning."

Our radar covered a radius of about fifty miles and there had not been a sighting of any vessel for better than a day, so it looked like it was not only going to be a beautiful week with no storms in sight but also a quiet patrol.

Just then, at the edge of the screen, I picked up something quite small. It was smaller than we normally would see this far from shore, where most vessels were in the fifty-foot-plus range. This was on the order of thirty feet or less, so it was definitely something to investigate.

The officer of the day (OOD) asked for a course to intercept, which took a moment to calculate since the other vessel was steaming due east at about ten knots while our vessel doing about twenty knots (to all the young people who hate geometry, it does have a use!). Calculating the intercept, I gave the new course to the OOD, and he gave the instruction, "Make it so."

It took us a few hours to reach the small object. As we approached we realized that it was actually a small cabin cruiser. A cabin cruiser of this size would normally only have a range of about 200 to 300 miles, and here we were, nearly 300 miles from shore!

As we approached, we saw on the deck of the small vessel what appeared to be a woman in her mid-thirties and her two small children. On the bridge was a man in his middle to late thirties. We tried to hail them. After we sounded the horn, the OOD grabbed the bullhorn, stepped to the edge of the bridge, and asked, "Ahoy there, can we be of assistance?"

The man on the bridge smiled and waved to our cutter.

The OOD asked him if he knew where he was. Meanwhile we could see the woman's expression as she gathered the two children under her arms. Have you ever seen somebody realize for the first time that something must be terribly wrong, but they have no clue as to what it could be? This was her expression.

But the man on the bridge of the small craft was still smiling and acting as if nothing was wrong. He responded with, "We are just out for an afternoon cruise. We should be back in the port in twenty or thirty minutes."

Given that it was flat calm and we could easily see twenty miles in all directions, and given that he was only traveling at ten knots an hour, I'm not sure what he was thinking. If he were truly twenty minutes from shore, we would have been looking at it straight ahead … but the only thing straight ahead of *his* position was the coast of Portugal!

The OOD asked them to heave to, meaning to stop, so that we might board. Now the man's look resembled that of his wife.

Our boarding party lowered the small boat and made their way to the side of his vessel. When they arrived, the man asked if there was a problem. Perhaps he thought that we believed they were carrying some kind of contraband.

The boarding crew told him that he was located 300 miles due east of Boston and that there was no way he could reach shore on his own. It looked like the young mother was going to faint as she started to cry.

It turned out that the man had rented the small craft for a cruise and had taken his family out from Marblehead Harbor to see the ocean and do a little fishing. They had drifted for a while, but by the time they decided it was time to go home, they could not see land.

Still, the craft was equipped with a compass, so knowing that they had gone straight out into the ocean, the man had figured that if he cruised westerly he would reach shore somewhere.

The only problem was no one had ever shown him how to use a compass. When you look at one, you can read it two ways: the correct way, and the way that is 180 degrees off of the correct way (when I have taught orienteering to young Pathfinders, a common mistake is to read the backside of the compass)!

We brought his small craft alongside us and used a set of lifeboat davits to raise his vessel onto ours. Making our way to Marblehead, we delivered Gilligan and his crew back to shore.

How often we go through life without learning how to use the compass! The Bible gives us instructions and the resources to steer a course that Jesus directs, but if we never open that book, we will never know how to maneuver!

Compass use requires instruction and practice; life requires instruction and prayer.

CHAPTER 31: HIGH WATER

For He shall give His angels charge over you, to keep you in all your ways. (Ps. 91:11)

I've had young people tell me that God no longer does miracles. The truth of the matter is that miracles are happening all around us. We just need to be aware and look around!

When I was seventeen years of age, I received my driver's license. Of course this entailed driver's education classes, driving with your parents, and (like any seventeen-year-old) taking any opportunity to get behind the wheel.

At the time, my family was living on Sconticut Neck in Fairhaven, Massachusetts. Living at home were my parents and five children: my brother, who is older than I am, two brothers younger than I am, one sister, and me. My older sister was away at the time.

Our home was located three-quarters of the way down the neck, adjacent to a dairy farm. We were about half a mile from the water on one side and just a few hundred yards from the water on the other side.

Chapter 31: High Water

I spent a good portion of my teenage years at this location. The only drawback was the fact that there was only one way on or off of the neck, and the New Bedford Bridge is one of those movable bridges that opens for boat traffic to the inner harbor, so it was not unusual to be delayed getting across (the only other way to New Bedford at that time was to go miles inland, to a narrower point of the Acushnet River, and that required not only a lot of time but a lot of gas).

My mother worked for New Bedford St. Luke's Hospital, which required crossing over the bridge each morning and evening (today they have a dike, which was built to protect New Bedford Harbor and prevent situations such as the one I'm about to describe). My father worked as a machinist, also in New Bedford.

On this particular morning, the weather report was predicting hurricane force winds. That's it! Unlike today, we didn't have the opportunity to watch storm radar showing the development of what was to come. Father had left for work early, and the schools had been closed, so we kids were all home, but my mother suspected that she might have difficulty getting to work. She asked if I would drive her in our car.

I jumped at the opportunity, not because I was anxious to see the storm but because it was a chance to drive! Mother placed my older brother in charge of the kids while she was gone, and we left.

As we proceeded up the neck, we saw the water getting closer and closer to the road. About one-quarter of the way from the top of the neck was the narrowest point, and it often was flooded, but when we arrived we discovered that, although the water was close to the road, it was still passable.

Visibility was very poor, and the rain was ferocious, but fortunately there was little to no traffic. We continued on towards New Bedford.

Just before the bridge on the left-hand side was the old footbridge, or causeway, that was used in the days of Joseph Bates, one of the eighteenth-century founders of the Adventist church. I was always fascinated by the stories of Joseph Bates. As we passed it, I took my eyes off the road, just imagining what it must have been like in the early 1800s. I know, taking my eyes off the road was a dumb thing to do; but then again, I was only seventeen.

In that split second, my mother screamed *"STOP!"*

As I slammed on the brakes, I looked forward. I saw that the water had risen above the base of the bridge and was only a few hundred feet in front of us. Now I could see why the traffic had been so light: there was no way that you could cross the bridge when it was underwater!

We sat there contemplating what our next move would be. My mother finally said that we might as well return home and wait the storm out (it was now also apparent that my father probably would not make it home that night). Making a U-turn on Route 6, I headed back to Sconticut Neck and home.

> In that split second, my mother screamed "STOP!"

It had only been about twenty minutes since we left the neck, so we did not anticipate there being any major problems. But when we arrived to that narrow low point, we could see that the water had already covered the road.

It now appeared we would not get back home either. One of the things they always taught us in driver's education, especially those living in and around the ocean, was that you should never drive into standing water. Remembering that instruction, I stopped and looked to my mother to see what we ought to do next.

I could tell by her expression that she was getting increasingly upset and anxious. She looked at me and told me to drive through the water, because she was going to get home to the rest of her family no matter what the obstacle might be.

At this point I would like to comment on the text at the beginning of the story. I quoted Psalm 91:11, but now I want to read verse 12: "In *their* hands they shall bear you up, lest you dash your foot against a stone."

We started to enter the water. I could tell that at some point it might be fairly deep, because it stretched for several hundred feet. Fortunately, the road was very straight and I could see where it came out at the other end. Using this as a guide I continued forward, focusing on that point (this is a technique that we often use with small motorboats in order to steer in a straight line).

As I focused on that far point, I noticed to the left and to the right of me the tops of several cars! I was getting worried because the water was up to the top of their windows, which meant that we ought to be in the same situation.

Yet there was no water coming in the door … and the level appeared to be well below my window … which could only mean that I was riding at least three feet above the road!

When we came out the other side, I stopped and asked my mother if she had seen what I saw. At that point she bowed her head and prayed, thanking God for lifting us up.

Yes, miracles still do happen, and angels still come to our aid. I have told this story on many occasions, and in each instance I have given God the glory.

God did not save my mother and me because we were any different than anyone else. We knew that there was nothing we could have done except witness His grace and glory. Miracles happen for His glory, and they are one tool that He uses to help all of us understand whose side He is on!

Each event and each story is unique. They are told to let everyone know the glory of a loving Savior. He gave His life so that we could have life; He suffered and died so we would not have to do the same!

CHAPTER 32: KING COBRA!

You shall tread upon the lion and the cobra, the young lion and the serpent you shall trample underfoot. Because he has set his love upon Me, therefore I will deliver him; I will set him on high, because he has known My name. He shall call upon Me, and I will answer him; I *will be* with him in trouble; I will deliver him and honor him. With a long life I will satisfy him, and show him My salvation. (Ps. 91:13-16)

Continuing from the verse of the previous story, we see that God is offering more than just deliverance. You will notice that He says that He will deliver us because we have set our love upon Him and because we know Him.

While on a business trip in Thailand, I had the opportunity to go into the rainforest. I was warned that there were many dangers and that I must never leave the path between the villages. Since it was broad daylight, I did not think that there would be much problem in the short distance between the two villages. I was not sure why they were so emphatic about staying on the path, but I did.

I was fascinated by the jungle around me. I could hear the sounds of many animals; especially those pesky monkeys that always had a habit of stealing my lunch.

About a quarter mile from the next village, I caught a glimpse of something black on the ground in front of me. I stopped about ten feet from the object, and as soon as I did, the head of the king cobra rose from the black pile to about four-and-a-half feet in the air and fanned its head in front of me.

Now I must say, I have always been fascinated by snakes. When I was young, my brother and I often caught them at home (that is, until we accidentally lost one in the house, and it was found by my grandmother!). I have an interesting scar on my small finger from a black racer that moved quicker than I could. So I'm aware that snakes can be quick!

This snake, however, was not a little black racer from back home. I had no doubt that it could get to me before I could turn and run. I leaned slightly to the left, and the snake followed me to the left. I leaned slightly to the right, and the snake repeated my action. There was no doubt in my mind that I was the object of the snake's concern ... he definitely was the object of my attention.

> *There was no doubt in my mind that I was the object of the snake's concern ... he definitely was the object of my attention.*

I felt like the best thing that I could do was to stay as still as possible and not give this serpent any indication that I was a threat. We stood and looked at each other for a few minutes. At last its head deflated, and the snake lowered to the ground and slithered off into the brush. I stayed put without moving for several more minutes just to be sure that he had plenty of time to get out of the way. I knew that I was no match for a king cobra, just as I know that I'm no match for the devil!

In an earlier story I quoted James chapter 4, verses 7 and 8a. It bears repeating: "Therefore submit to God. Resist the devil and he will flee from you. Draw near to God and He will draw near to you." As I said, we cannot resist the devil on our own. The way to resist the devil is by submitting to God. Our duty is not to try harder but to draw near to God, and He will draw near to us.

I finally proceeded down that pathway, much more aware of my surroundings and much more conscious of every noise or movement.

Just a few hundred feet from where I had seen the king cobra, I noticed a family: mother, father, and baby having a picnic lunch in the brush. I stopped and told them what I had seen. They just smiled.

I'm not sure if they even understood English, but they did not seem very concerned about their surroundings. It's interesting that when we don't understand the warning, we don't realize the danger; and if we don't realize the danger, then we place ourselves in peril!

Much of the world is unconcerned about their surroundings, so God has given us the mission of telling them about a Savior who died so that they might spend eternity with Him. I have never quite understood why Jesus has chosen to use people to reach people. As an engineer it just does not seem logical … but then again, it's not a matter of logic but of love!

God also wants *us* to be aware of our surroundings rather than oblivious to the wiles of the devil. We live in a pretty sinful world, and there are issues all around us that demand our attention; but they also shouldn't distract us from our love of our Savior.

CHAPTER 33: OHIO ROAD TRIP

My son, do not forget my law, but let your heart keep my commands; for length of days and long life and peace they will add to you. (Prov. 3:1, 2)

While I was working as an engineer in Fort Wayne, Indiana, my brother-in-law moved from Columbus, Ohio, to upstate New York. He still had a number of household items in his former home, and I agreed to retrieve them for safe keeping. My small station wagon, a little Datsun, did not hold very much, but I did have a trailer hitch which would allow me to rent a small U-Haul and pick up everything that he needed. My oldest daughter was about ten years old and wanted to come along for the ride, so the two of us headed out across the wondrous flatlands of Indiana and Ohio.

For the most part, the roads were fairly straight, and you could tell how far you were from the center of the next town by the number of the road. For instance, the road labeled 50N was actually half a mile north of the center of the nearest town. Not a very complex system, but it did come in handy from time to time.

The highways had a rather large crown which allowed for water to run off in those wonderful flatlands. On each side there was a substantial ditch to collect that runoff. I had once had to drive into such a ditch to avoid an accident. That was not a delightful experience, so I avoided the ditches at all costs.

I had spent a number of years in the Midwest by then, but I never totally got used to the flat terrain. As we started to get closer to Ohio, I must say that the monotony became worse. The one difference from Indiana was that there were slightly rolling hills, but still nothing that compared with my beloved New England.

We had been on the road for several hours and were nearing our destination when we came to the crest of one of those rolling hills. As we approached the crest, we could see down the other side. We could also see two tractor-trailers coming toward us side-by-side!

> *With my eyes closed, I offered a prayer. I decided it probably was better to not see what was about to happen.*

One was passing the other, and there could not have been any more than two feet between the trucks. Likewise there was no more than two feet on either side of the trucks due to the ditches.

My oldest daughter had that typical reaction of covering her face and screaming. I never understood the advantage of covering her face or the benefit of screaming, but there she was! Of course, I acted in a much more adult manner: I gripped the steering wheel, aimed for the two-foot gap between the trucks, and did what every brave man would do in a similar situation ... I shut my eyes!

With my eyes closed, I offered a prayer. I decided it probably was better to not see what was about to happen.

The text in Proverbs I started this chapter with is not about doing but about being. God tells us not to forget His law, not so that we will always be *doing* the right thing; rather, He tells us to let our hearts keep His commands.

Just what is your heart but the center of love? The story of Jesus and of the Bible as a whole is a story of love, not one of obligation or duty.

As I was praying with my eyes closed, I could hear the trucks coming closer ... and eventually passing.

I opened my eyes to find that we were on the other side of those two trucks! We had somehow passed through the eye of the needle. There is no way that the three of us could have fit on the road at the same time, yet neither truck had gone off into the ditch. In the rearview mirror, I could see them pass over the top of the hill.

We pulled over at the next available spot and offered a prayer of thanks to a gracious and loving God. We were shaking for some time, but we had no doubt that the angels had been with us once again.

God promises to give us a long life, but greatest of all is His promise to grant His peace to us.

CHAPTER 34: SHOT ACROSS THE BOW

> For the grace of God that brings salvation has appeared to all men, teaching us that, denying ungodliness and worldly lusts, we should live soberly, righteously, and godly in the present age … (Titus 2:11, 12)

I'm going to break Titus 2:11-13 into two sections with two different stories. This story relates to verses 11 and 12; the next will relate to verse 13.

This is truly a powerful text. Though it appears as if it is telling us that our salvation is about what we do, the fact is that it is doing just the opposite. God does not expect us to change, for He is well aware that we cannot. It is rather that His instruction and guidance allow us to deny ungodliness and worldly lusts! The truth is that He loves us too much to leave us the way He finds us!

There are times when we need a wake-up call; when we need to be brought back to an understanding of the sinful world that we live in.

Chapter 34: Shot Across the Bow

Life seemed to be going well. I was running a company out of Alexandria, Virginia, while living in New Hampshire. The owner of the business had approached me and encouraged me to develop a new enterprise in a growing niche of the plasma industry. In a matter of just three years, we had tapped into this particular industry and developed sales totaling several million dollars. The only problem was that I was just an employee. If I was ever going to secure something for my future, I needed to have ownership.

Then another entrepreneur offered me 49% of a new startup at the three-year point!

As much as I hated to leave the first company, I knew that this new one would succeed. Plus, by starting again, I would in fact be able to set up my retirement nest egg. Leaving the first company and going to the new venture had yet another advantage: it was based out of Billerica, Massachusetts. This was only an hour and a half from my home in New Hampshire. So once again, I started off into a new venture.

Just a few months into the establishment of the company, I discovered a lump on my side. Like most people when they first discover such things, I ignored it. However, I was "disadvantaged" in that my mother, father, sister, and one of my brothers were all in the medical field (which means that you're not allowed to ignore these things). Following their suggestions, I went to a doctor to have it checked out.

> *Just a few months into the establishment of the company, I discovered a lump on my side.*

I told the doctor to move quickly, because I had a startup company to get off the ground. He took a biopsy and told me to lay low until he got the results. My idea of taking it easy was to have my side taped, then go to my lecture in Minneapolis.

Somehow, I do not think abusing our bodies in order to be successful is what God intended. We are to live soberly, righteously, and godly in the present age, and with respect for the temple of God. We should not push it with a 100- to 120-hour work week. God does not expect us to live for work but to work so that we can live for Him.

It was apparent that I needed a wake-up call; for this life is not about the job that we have but about the mission which we are to perform.

It didn't take too many days for me to realize that going to Minneapolis was a major mistake. After I gave my lecture, but before the end of the seminar, I came home. As soon as I got there, I received a call from the doctor asking me to see him as soon as possible. As my wife and I sat in his office, he used the dreaded "C" word.

A thousand things ran through my mind. I must have looked like I was off in space. And when he told me that they had to conduct some more tests to try to determine how to treat my condition, I did not show much emotion. I was trying to decide what I was going to do next, for he had just told me that I had both Hodgkin's and non-Hodgkin's lymphoma ... simultaneously.

Each of these conditions was known to have different treatments. The doctors were not sure exactly how to proceed. They had to do one more test, a gallium scan, to determine the extent of the problem. But it just happened to be Memorial Day weekend.

The doctor wanted to get the test scheduled as soon as possible. He told me to go home and stay by the phone. He said that his secretary would call with the timing for the test. I just smiled and nodded. He said he realized that I probably was in shock over the news and that we would talk again in a day or two.

I explained that I was not in shock. As an engineer I was accustomed to weighing my options. I said I'd known many engineers, and that we tended to think the same way: that is, cause-and-effect.

I then told him about my childhood hero, Captain Joseph Bates, who was a 19th century evangelist. Captain Bates was once preaching an evangelistic series somewhere near Chesapeake Bay. While he was preaching, some rabble-rousers entered the back of the church with hot tar and a rail.

He saw them come in and stopped his sermon. He addressed them, saying that he knew what they were up to and that if God was through with him, then he would just as soon spend the rest of the time until He came at the bottom of the Chesapeake. However, he told them, if God was not through with him, then they could not touch him!

Chapter 34: Shot Across the Bow

It is said that they sat down and were converted before the end of that day.

I told the doctor that I knew, like my childhood hero Captain Bates, that if God was done with me, then all the odds in the world wouldn't help me pull through. But if He was not done, I would not only pull through but come out stronger than before!

We then went home and waited, and waited, and waited. My wife kept telling me to call, but I said, "No, they said to wait, so I'm waiting."

However, at 4:30 p.m. it became apparent that the call was not forthcoming. I called the doctor's secretary to find out what was going on.

When I explained the situation to her, she said, "Oh, my goodness! I forgot all about setting up your test. Now I'll have to wait until after the holiday! You don't understand the day that I've had!"

I thought my wife was going to crawl through the phone and grab that secretary by the throat! The day she had? We had just been told that I had less than a 50% chance of survival, and *she* had a bad day?!

However, if there's one word that describes Christ, it is compassion. Jesus tells us in Matthew 5:44, "But I say to you, love your enemies, bless those who curse you, do good to those who hate you, and pray for those who spitefully use you and persecute you." Our first reaction in many situations is to strike out, but God would have us to love and pray. We need to be aware of the need to treat all of our brothers and sisters with the utmost of compassion.

I eventually had the gallium test and we went back to the doctor's office.

I had previously told him that I had done some research and discovered that the majority of people who had radiation treatment ended up with another form of cancer. Although he had agreed with me, he had informed me, "At least you get rid of the one that you have."

I had found this to be small comfort. If I were to develop another form of cancer, I said, I wouldn't have "succeeded." I would do the chemo but not the radiation.

He had said he would be insistent unless I was in the advanced stages.

Now as we met post-gallium test, he informed me that I had gotten my wish: the tests had shown that the cancer was in multiple lymph nodes throughout my body. They would not be able to radiate my entire body. They would have to rely on chemotherapy alone.

The problem now was to determine the cocktail. Non-Hodgkin's and Hodgkin's treatments were totally different, and their fear was that if they treated one, the other would kill me. They opted for the more aggressive treatment, targeting the non-Hodgkin's Lymphoma.

There were many people who had told me that I should not take any treatment but only rely on faith. However, I had met others who had refused treatment until it was too late. I didn't want that to happen.

I hold faith highly. At the same time, as a scientist, I was convinced that perhaps God led the hands of the doctors who developed the different treatments. As such, I was going to give it a try. And so the excitement began.

Someone who has not experienced being told that they have cancer may have a hard time understanding why I made these decisions. Looking back, I believe I would have done the same thing over again. Since then I have had renal cancer where my right kidney was removed, and also a brain tumor that was removed (believe it or not) through my nose! We do not have all the medical answers, but I'm willing to work with what we do have.

As the treatments began, I questioned my standing with God. Like most people who experience that first announcement that they have cancer, I began with one simple word: *why?* Or, more specifically, *why me?*

You first review your life and wonder if it is something that you did, or if you caused it to happen. Goodness knows I had been exposed to enough things in my life to have caused at least one of the lymphomas, and I had enough darkness to deserve the wrath of God.

Then you begin to ask if it is because you are not close enough to your Lord; you begin to doubt your own faith.

After prayer and supplication, it begins to take shape: the simple fact that we live in a sinful world, and thus sinful things happen!

Also, as I have mentioned before, the Bible clearly tells us that God directs our steps. So there had to be a reason God was allowing this to

Chapter 34: Shot Across the Bow

happen. *All* things happen for a reason. Nothing happens by chance. Once I understood this; once I realized that no matter what happened, He was still in control and was leading in my life, I could move forward and try to understand the lesson I was meant to learn.

Just when I was beginning to adjust to the treatment (a treatment I would not wish on anybody), I started having severe reactions to one of the medications in the form of seizures. This forced me to search even deeper for the meaning that God had for me to learn.

I started a blog on the Internet called *The Cancer Weekly*. In it I took each new event and tried to draw something positive from what happened in the form of a Scriptural promise.

To print that blog in this publication would be, in effect, a book within a book. Instead I'll say that my intent at that time was to help anyone else who might have been experiencing the symptoms, complications, and troubles that I was experiencing; to let them know they were not alone.

When we have Jesus as our friend, no matter what we go through, no matter what we experience, He is there at our side. When He says, "I will never leave you nor forsake you" (Heb. 13:5), He is telling us the absolute truth, because He is the Way and the Truth.

They say hindsight is 20/20. Looking back on my life, I realize that God was trying to get my attention. He wanted more for my life than engineering and business success. He wanted my private life in order; He wanted me to put my focus on Him. He had to fire across my bow to get my attention.

That reminds me of another short tale before we move on.

Back in my Coast Guard days, when I was still on the ship, we would chase Russian spy ships until they were outside our twelve-mile limit. Then the day came when the U.S. decided to enforce a 200-mile limit around our coast.

Before then it had been a game of cat and mouse; chase but do not stop. Now the command had finally come through to put an end to this game! The captain was instructed that the next time we caught one of these ships within our waters, we were to board and seize the vessel.

We found one of these little "fishing vessels" (that never did any fishing) ten miles off the coast of New Hampshire. We knew they were there to monitor the activities of Pease Air Force Base. We immediately hailed them on the radio, telling them to heave to, an expression which means "stop and be boarded."

These small fishing vessels with one million antennas were not built like normal fishing vessels. When they decided to move out, they could do so and with great speed.

We followed in hot pursuit, but it didn't take us long to realize that we would never catch them. The captain gave the command to load the five-inch bow gun and place a round across the bow of the vessel.

There's just something about a five-inch explosive ordinance blowing up the ocean in front of you that gets your attention! The vessel stopped, and we boarded.

God knows how to get our attention. The problem we have is listening once He does! That experience you are complaining about? That problem in your life? It just might be God firing across your bow!

CHAPTER 35: PRAYER IS THE ANSWER

[L]ooking for the blessed hope and glorious appearing of our great God and Savior Jesus Christ .... (Titus 2:13)

Never belittle someone who is suffering while being treated for any condition! Unless you've walked a mile in their shoes, you don't know how real their suffering is.

There were many low points and side effects of my illness and treatment that I talked about in my blog, *The Cancer Weekly*. But no matter how low I felt, I managed; and God gave me the strength to come to Sabbath school and be with the youth.

There were fourteen in our youth group. I loved every one of them as if they were my own. There were times when I couldn't stand, and so I would work with them from my wheelchair. The youth always reached out to me; I knew they had hearts of compassion.

As soon as Sabbath school was over, my wife would transport me back home where I would collapse for two or three days before I was able to get out of bed again.

The youth were also a part of a group called the Mohawk Pathfinders. This was the year of the national camporee, but there was no way that I would be able to go. Still, I encouraged them to all attend for the experience.

While they were gone, I reached my lowest point in the chemo experience. I had had a continuous resting temperature of around 101 degrees for over three months, and my body was starting to give up. I could no longer walk or even rise from my bed. They placed me on hospice, assuming that I would not live beyond six months.

Discouragement once again raised its ugly head. I did not think I could hold out much longer. In my prayers I asked God for some hope. *Hope is a power, encouraged and strengthened by faith, lays hold upon future realities, standing upon the sure promises of God and inspired with the certainty of future possessions.* As I said in the first story in this book, I found this quote years ago in a sermon that my father had written and left for me. But it was only at this time in my life that I began to really understand what it meant.

> I went from depression to elation. I praised God for the hope that He had given me.

I prayed at 2 o'clock on a Sabbath afternoon. I remember the exact time, because at that moment I started to improve. Within a few hours I was able to sit up, and before the end of the day I was walking ... something that I had not thought would happen ever again. I went from depression to elation. I praised God for the hope that He had given me.

But that's only half of the story.

When the Pathfinders returned, they came to visit me. They told me how they had attempted to arrange for a miracle flight to bring me to the camporee. But since I was, of course, unable to even consider leaving my bed at the time, they had done the next best thing: at exactly 2:00 p.m. my time, 30,000 Pathfinders knelt in prayer on my behalf!

No one will ever be able to tell me that intercessory prayer does not work! In less than two months, all signs of both lymphomas were in remission. What a marvelous and wonderful God we have, and what a powerful tool we have in prayer!

Many years later I was relating this story to a group of juniors at a camp meeting. I saw one of the mothers start to cry. After the meeting I went over to her and asked if there was anything I could do to help and if I could have a prayer with her.

She wiped her eyes and told me that ten years earlier, she had been a Pathfinder at that very camporee. She had taken part in that prayer for a man who was suffering from cancer back in some town somewhere on the East Coast.

In her skepticism, she said, she had assumed that it was all made up to get the kids to focus on praying. She had never believed that there was a real situation to pray about.

Her tears were ones of sorrow and regret that she owed to God for not believing. They were also tears of understanding that, even though she had prayed without believing, a miracle still indeed happened!

All we can do is pray the prayer of the father in Mark chapter 9 who had a possessed son. Jesus said to him, "If you can believe, all things *are* possible to him who believes." The father responded, with tears in his eyes, "Lord, I believe; help my unbelief!" (Mark 9:17-24).

We know that God gives all people a measure of faith, and that this small measure is sufficient to accept Jesus Christ. Once we have accepted Him, He covers us with His robe of righteousness; and it is through His righteousness that we receive our salvation!

CHAPTER 36: HYDROGEN

The wind blows where it wishes, and you hear the sound of it, but cannot tell where it comes from and where it goes. So is everyone who is born of the Spirit. (John 3:8)

While developing systems in the plasma industry, I received many strange requests. Perhaps the strangest is the basis of the following story!

I have always been interested in science, and I was always fascinated by the stars and planets. My interest in astronomy had developed while doing celestial navigation in the Coast Guard (now before you go off the deep end, astronomy is not astrology!).

One afternoon my secretary forwarded a call to me from someone who was making inquiries about a unique application of plasma. The man did not get two words out before I knew exactly who I was speaking to.

Chapter 36: Hydrogen

Dr. Carl Sagan is one of the people that I had read about and observed on numerous television programs. You might say that he had a unique voice. It was easy to distinguish him amongst many others, and my interest was piqued.

The good doctor was inquiring about the possibility of a unique application for a specially-made plasma. He wished to analyze gases via a spectrometer.

Telescopes can pick up light being reflected from different planets. By analyzing this light, specifically by duplicating the light spectrum with the plasma, astronomers can determine the consistency of the atmosphere on a given planet.

Dr. Sagan wanted to know if I could make a plasma system with a quartz chamber in order to generate a pure hydrogen plasma. The process would involve evacuating the chamber to simulate the vacuum of space, injecting hydrogen gas at a low level into the chamber, and ionizing the gas with a plasma generator. It sounded so simple, but there was one caveat: hydrogen cannot be contained.

You might ask, "Why can it not be contained?" Hydrogen is such a small atom that it will leak even through a stainless steel container. In a quartz container, the leakage could be even higher. That is why, in most plasma applications, the hydrogen is mixed with another gas and is usually only a few percent of the total mixture.

I thought about the request while we were still on the phone. Finally I agreed to the idea under one condition: Dr. Sagan was to let me know in what state he was going to fire it up so I could be sure that I was far enough away. We both chuckled at that.

I proceeded to develop the system, but after he received the unit, he never contacted me again. I'm assuming that everything went well.

Hydrogen is a lot like the Holy Spirit in that it cannot be contained. A pastor once said, "Give me ten new Christians for every hundred old believers!" What he was implying was that those who have just received the Gospel are far more likely to share what they have received than those who are comfortable in their religion.

It really is all about Jesus. When we are filled with the Holy Spirit, we are filled with God's hydrogen … and we cannot contain what leaks out at every chance!

Wouldn't it be wonderful if the Holy Spirit overflowed onto everyone with whom we came into contact? The desire to have everyone experience the joy that fills our souls is the true meaning of a relationship with Jesus Christ.

CHAPTER 37: TRAINS AND TRESTLES

There is a way *that seems* right to a man, but its end *is* the way of death. (Prov. 16:25)

s a kid (and as an adult) I have done my share of dumb things. This story probably ranks right up there with the worst.

One hot summer afternoon, four of us were trying to figure out what trouble we could get into. At least we were trying to find something to pass the time. We had a set of tracks and a trestle near our house that went over the Nashua River, so someone suggested exploring inside the trestle.

We teens had no idea if there was a regular schedule or if it was strictly hit or miss because in the early 1960s, railroads were on the decline. Passenger trains had long since disappeared in the area, and trains in general were few and far between.

I probably should have assumed that there was a regular schedule. In addition, we had been told never to play on the railroad tracks. But when you say "never" or "no" to a teenager, it is processed as, "Do it as soon as possible." Not only would this be something we were not supposed to be doing, it might actually be interesting! So we decided to give it a go.

There was a tie missing on the trestle. The only way into the trestle was to go through that gap, which was located about halfway across the river. I was still the skinniest one in the group, so I went down first, then I moved to one side to let the others follow.

After about forty-five minutes of exploration, the newness had worn off. And we were beginning to get a little apprehensive about the river underneath us.

The color of the Nashua River and the smell associated with that color were determined by the pollution provided by the Leominster plastics factories upstream. The water was blue one day, red another day, and a slimy brown on the days in between. We had no idea as to how deep it was because we could never see to the bottom, and the banks were covered with a paper-like paste. Nothing was living in that river.

> *When I was about waist high through the opening, I saw the train ... just about thirty feet away!*

Since that time, local townspeople have enforced concern for environmental issues, and the river is actually supporting life once again, but back then pollution not only existed but thrived. This day it was in one of its blue phases, and the smell was disgusting. We envisioned what would happen to our flesh were we to actually fall in.

Like many teens with short attention spans, we were done with this diversion. Again, since I was the smallest, I was the first one to begin to climb out of the trestle.

When I was about waist high through the opening, I saw the train ... just about thirty feet away!

I certainly would not be able to outrun it going forward, and there was no place to go in the other direction, because the train was already starting to cross the trestle. I let out a yell to the others to hold on, then I dropped down, wrapping my arms around one of the ties.

Not only did the train seem to go on forever, but the vibration prevented me from supporting myself in any other way than holding on to the railroad tie.

The train finally passed, and we were able to climb off the trestle. I suppose it was an experience to see the train from the bottom side … but it was an experience I did not ever wish to repeat!

People both young and old often try to find their own diversions. Many of the things that we do, we do without considering whether they are right or wrong.

I remember a friend once telling me that she actually believed that all people were basically good inside. Well, when we don't have a relationship with Jesus, our choices are based on what people call their "inner voice," and the Bible makes it clear that the heart is full of deceit.

The verse at the start of this story explains this as simply as can be: we cannot truly determine right without God's input. This is just one more reason why a relationship with Jesus Christ is essential.

CHAPTER 38: STATE OF THE DEAD

> As God lives, *who* has taken away my justice, and the Almighty, *who* has made my soul bitter, as long as my breath *is* in me, and the breath of God in my nostrils, my lips will not speak wickedness, nor my tongue utter deceit. Far be it from me that I should say you are right; till I die I will not put away my integrity from me. My righteousness I hold fast, and will not let it go; my heart shall not reproach *me* as long as I live. (Job 27:2-6)

I was not overly shy as a young man. As a matter of fact, all too often my mouth engaged before my brain. I remember attending a special training by the National Organization of Victims Assistance (NOVA). In this course we were instructed how to be first responders in the event of a major catastrophe. There were fourteen pastors in the class, and the instructor was not happy. He informed us that teaching this course to pastors was always difficult. The reason why was that pastors had great difficulty keeping their mouths shut!

I'm not sure if that was good or bad. There is a time to speak and a time to be silent. Knowing the difference between the two is the work of a lifetime. When it comes to our faith, discerning which of these two times it is can make the difference between death and eternal life.

While studying electrical engineering at Andrews University, I worked at a company in Fort Wayne, Indiana. Because of my background in the military and the courses I had already completed, I was given the title of electrical engineer before completing my degree.

Thus, even though I had just one year to finish, I began to question the need to complete the program. And though I had not made the announcement, I had already planned in my heart to shift to theology. This would mean that I would start down yet another path, extending my undergraduate training for at least two more years. I began taking as many religion courses as I could.

At the same time, my wife and I had been talking about moving back to New England. It became apparent that the only way to accomplish this was to just do it!

My in-laws lived in Lancaster, Massachusetts, the home of Atlantic Union College. As you will recall, I had attended Atlantic Union prior to going into the service. All those years ago, my

A homecoming of sorts: me in my senior year, in 1982 at Atlantic Union College.

major fields of study had been art and mathematics. Now, all of the courses that I had taken at both Andrews and Atlantic Union could combine toward my degree. So I resigned from my engineering position in Michigan, and we loaded up the U-Haul truck and headed for Massachusetts. We moved in with my in-laws, and I secured a position as chief engineer of a small microwave development company. I then re-enrolled in classes at Atlantic Union.

After several months in my new position, I discovered that there were about fifteen employees meeting on every lunch break for a

Bible study. It was a nondenominational Bible study led by one of the technicians in the lab. He asked if I was interested in joining.

After giving it much thought, I decided to join but to say as little as possible. I felt it would be awkward if, as their boss, I injected too much into their discussion.

The leader of the group knew that I was not only a Seventh day Adventist but studying to become a pastor, but he chose not to mention this to the others, for which I was thankful. The studies progressed for over a month, and I found them enriching. There were many times that I almost spoke up, but I held myself back.

The day that the discussion shifted to the state of the dead, I knew that if I spoke, there would be problems. But then, as the study was coming to a close, the leader held up his hand and looked right at me. He said, "Ron, you are a Seventh day Adventist, and I know you believe somewhat differently than what we have been discussing."

This caught me totally off guard, and I just nodded yes.

He then asked if I would give them a quick overview of what I believed in the closing ten minutes of their discussion.

There was no way that I could begin to explain perhaps *only* the most controversial of our beliefs in ten minutes. Thinking that I could dodge the bullet, I told them there was just not enough time.

I think he might have been planning something all along, because he smiled and said, "Then why don't you take the entire time tomorrow, and let us know just how different your ideas are?"

God directs our steps and places us in positions to do His will. There are no accidents, no coincidences, and no missed opportunities if we listen to His prodding.

I could refuse and back down or submit to the opportunity. I had not done many Bible studies, but I did know what I believed: I believed in the Bible and the Bible alone. Sensing that it was out of my hands, I said, "I will need the entire forty-five minutes tomorrow, and undoubtedly we will be covering the subject from Genesis to Revelation."

What had I gotten myself into this time? (For the record, I would never suggest starting a series of Bible studies with the state of the dead!)

I went home that night and spent time on my knees. With the Bible before me, I wrote down a series of texts. What I was going to present

Chapter 38: State of The Dead

would probably not be well received, and yet I knew God must be glorified.

The truth makes people feel uncomfortable. The truth often makes *us* feel uncomfortable. Yet we were commissioned to share that same truth. It is never to be used for argument or as a club to browbeat because, really, the truth is a Man, not a list of facts! I realize that the truth is sharper than any two-edged sword, and yet it was given to us by the source of all love. When used with love, it slices to the heart without destroying the body. When used without love, it slices the body *and* destroys the heart. God will let us know the difference!

When we came together the next day, I asked them all to turn to 2 Timothy 3:16. I then informed them, "This text says all Scripture is given by inspiration of God. Therefore, I am going to use both the New and the Old Testaments in this discussion."

I also informed them that I was not going to attempt to tear down or malign their discussions from the last few days. What I was presenting was from the Bible and the Bible alone and was not of any unique interpretation. I would do little more than read texts and ask them for their thoughts on those texts. They all appeared to be comfortable with this approach.

The first text was Genesis 2:7: "And the Lord God formed man *of* the dust of the ground, and breathed into his nostrils the breath of life; and man became a living being." After a brief discussion, they agreed that man was a combination of the breath of life and a body formed from the dust of the earth.

The second text was Romans 6:23: "For the wages of sin *is* death, but the gift of God *is* eternal life in Christ Jesus our Lord." I asked, "How do we obtain eternal life?" The unanimous answer was that it was a gift from God.

I then asked, "What is sin?" After several comments I took the others through an understanding of 1 John 3:4, 1 John 4:8, and Matthew 22:40, showing them that the law and love were synonymous (I would suggest to the reader to look up these and the texts to come and follow the progression).

From there I showed that sin was about a failed relationship with God. "Sin is lawlessness, and lawlessness is godlessness." This process took fifteen of our minutes, and the clock was ticking.

From here we went to Psalm 6:5, Ecclesiastes 9:5, Psalm 146:3 and 4, Job 19:23 and 26, and Ezekiel 18:4. The group was beginning to mumble and show signs of discomfort. One finally asked when we were going to look at the New Testament.

So we turned immediately to 1 Thessalonians 4:15 and 16, followed by 1 Corinthians 15:51-57. Shifting gears, we turned to John chapter 11. Here we read how Jesus himself referred to death as sleep. Then we jumped to 1 Timothy 6:16 and discussed how God alone was immortal.

Moving to Acts chapter 2, we saw that David, a man after Jesus's own heart, was still in the grave. Shifting to 2 Timothy 4:7 and 8, we saw that Paul expects to remain in the grave until Christ's return. My final text was Revelation 22:12, and the room broke into chaos.

By doing little more than reading a series of texts and letting them interpret those texts, we had threatened eternal hell, the secret rapture, life after death, purgatory, and the security of much of their lifelong beliefs.

The Bible study was over (in fact, as long as I worked at that small microwave engineering company, it never resumed). Several cursed me as they left. My worst fears had materialized, and I began to wonder how we were going to function in the future.

However, one man stayed behind that day. He started to weep, then he looked at me and said, "It now all makes sense. I have never felt comfortable with the idea of my mother being in heaven or seeing the problems that I've gone through!"

He then proceeded to tell me how his mother had passed away when he was a small child and how he had been raised in an orphanage. He asked me if we could study more together.

We did study, and then I invited him to a Revelation seminar that was beginning nearby. By the end of that seminar, the man was baptized. Today he serves as an elder in the church near his home.

God has given us a commission to spread His Word and share the love of Jesus Christ. As we strengthen our relationship with Him, He will prod us to help us distinguish when we are to speak and when we are to remain silent.

We must never forget His commission, and time is too short to postpone the need to speak up. Literally millions of people are waiting to hear this message. We cannot wait until we are in our comfort zone to tell it.

CHAPTER 39: CANCER AGAIN

He has shown you, O man, what *is* good; and what does the Lord require of you but to do justly, to love mercy, and to walk humbly with your God? (Micah 6:8)

In the story of my first bout with cancer, I left off with the miraculous recovery initiated by intercessory prayer. That was not the end of that story, for I still was not listening to God and following His story for my life.

After my recovery, I returned to my startup company. It had struggled in its first year, but by the time we approached the three-year spinoff point, we already exceeded $6 million in sales per year. The owner realized that, according to our contract, we would separate the plasma division of the company and I would receive 49%!

Some people have a hard time letting go of assets, even when those assets were the responsibility of someone else. The owner was faced with having to turn over $3 million a year in equity to me. So two months before the contract date, he came to me and stated that he could not do it. He would rather kill the enterprise than surrender 49%; and with 51% he had the ability to starve the endeavor to spin off the plasma division into a new company.

(What I was unaware of at the time was that he had taken steps to ensure his success by starting a new company in Taiwan. This new company was utilizing the technology that I had developed. They even had schematics with my name still in the legend. How do you compete with yourself?)

> Sometimes God has to take you to the edge of the precipice before you begin to see the light.

The conversation left me with two choices: take the battle to court or walk away. If I were to take the battle to court, I believed that I would win. However, at least thirty-five people would have been out of work before victory could be realized! God has called us to do justly. He tells us that justice and vengeance are His; we are not supposed to retaliate or seek vengeance in any way.

It was not an easy decision to walk away from everything that I had built, but the people who were employed there had become my friends. I could not see punishing them for my gain, so I handed the owner my keys and walked away.

What was I to do now? There were not many companies to choose from that used the application of plasma with which I worked (six, to be exact). The first, where I had been general manager, was still operating. The second business, which I had started in Virginia, was still operating. Now this third company in the same industry was going to continue to operate. Altogether I had started or already been involved in four of the six companies, so my remaining options were limited.

So in February 2001, I decided to become a consultant. This way I would build two pieces of equipment in a one-man shop. Additionally, if I was the engineer, the assembler, and the salesman, no one but me would suffer if I did not succeed. By September of that same year, I had done $250,000 worth of consulting and engineering.

Then, on September 11, 2001, my next wake-up call happened, and my life, like so many, forever changed. My wife and I had just left my little office in Troy, New Hampshire, when we heard about the attack on the Twin Towers in New York City. All air travel came to a stop, and all equipment purchases came to a temporary halt.

Sometimes God has to take you to the edge of the precipice before you begin to see the light. Because you are successful in one area, it does not mean that is what God wants you to do. How was I to walk humbly with God?

I had no idea when or if things would resume, but I did have mouths to feed. I prayed about what I was to do, and I began to realize that God had some plan for me other than electrical engineering.

Back in February my wife had begun working with an autistic young lady. I had seen that the work, while not lucrative, was very personally rewarding, so I now closed down my office and also started working with special needs programs.

It required a major adjustment to our lifestyle and resulted in an income that was one-third of what we had been earning. But happiness is not a coefficient of more income. It's interesting to note that if you make more money, you just spend more money!

After working in this field for a few months, I decided to see if I could get into a management position. My master's degree was an MS in business management with an emphasis in human relations, so it would be applicable to almost any management-centered occupation.

I began distributing resumés and received a call fairly quickly from an agency looking for an operations manager. It was obvious that I was overqualified for the position, but I assured the company that I would not leave as soon as something better developed.

I was eager to do as well as I possibly could. My first approach was to study all of the state rules and regulations. But it did not take me long to realize that the company I was working for was not following those regulations.

I began to point out some of the areas that were being violated, but I was soon told to just sign the papers and keep quiet. This presented a moral dilemma: how did I reconcile omissions that were causing harm to the very people I was supposed to be serving? Then, not long after

Chapter 39: Cancer Again

I started working there, the state approached me and requested the information I'd discovered.

I struggled with this job situation for several years. Jesus instructs us to do justly, to love mercy, and to walk humbly with our God. I even told my wife that I was not sure if I could continue.

Meanwhile, at the beginning of December 2003, I noticed what felt like a kidney stone. I had had one of those in the past, and it was not a pleasant experience. I got an ultrasound and then a CAT scan, then my wife and I went in to see the doctor about one week before Christmas.

To our shock, the doctor started to talk about surgery on Christmas Eve! Confused, I asked him what he was talking about: I was not aware of a surgical procedure to remove kidney stones.

Apparently there had been a lapse in communications. The doctor informed me that my right kidney was cancerous and needed to be removed. There were tumors on the left kidney as well, but those did not seem to be a problem. The left kidney was at least working at 60% efficiency.

It had only been four years since my last experience with cancer, and this blow wasn't softened by previous experience. I told the doctor that I would not put my family through a Christmas Eve like he was suggesting. If I had already had the cancer for a while, it could stay there until after the new year.

On January 4, 2004, I had my right kidney removed. It would take three months of recuperation before I would be allowed back to work.

During this time the company asked if I would resign. I had created too many headaches for them, and they wanted to take advantage of my situation. However, I had already been granted medical leave, so I refused the request. I knew that since I had been granted leave, they could not fire me. I had a few months to determine what I was going to do. In the meantime I'd be able to collect short-term disability.

Then I received a call from the State of New Hampshire, telling me that based on the information I had provided and their review of the records, the agency which I had been working for would be closed on February 29. This was going to be a surprise, so they asked that I not inform the company.

I knew that once they closed the doors, it would be difficult to retrieve my personal items from my office, so I went to the building and removed them. A short while later, I was informed that there was a warrant for my arrest.

I called the Peterborough Police Department to find out what this was all about. The detective told me that the warrant was for breaking and entering into the company. It also reported that I had removed numerous items. I asked what those items were, and he said, "Your personal effects."

I then asked him, "If I had the master key and the card to swipe at the door, why would it be considered breaking and entering? Technically, I was still the operations manager of the company, even though I was on medical leave."

The company had known that I had been there because the key card swipe system notified them when I entered and when I left. They had also noted that the only items missing were my personal effects. However, I am sure they were actually concerned that I may have downloaded incriminating evidence from the computer. They had changed all the passcodes on the computers after I left, but I had once demonstrated (when a secretary had left unannounced) that someone could still access the computer files through Windows.

But I had not touched the computers, so I had nothing to fear.

The police officer told me that the charges would be dropped. And the state did close that agency. But that is not the end of the story, as I was not yet pursuing the path onto which God would eventually lead me.

CHAPTER 40: PASTOR FINALLY

But seek first the kingdom of God and His righteousness, and all these things shall be added to you. (Matt. 6:33)

The termination of the company by the state of New Hampshire closed a door, and I wondered if I would ever go through it again. But then in the beginning of March 2004, I received a call from the state agency that managed all private disability agencies in the southwest corner of New Hampshire. They asked if I could be involved in establishing a new agency which would deal with the personnel that previously had been managed by the closed one. Seeing this as an opportunity to do it the correct way, I agreed to be involved.

However, I soon learned that unjust and improper practices were not restricted to the former company. After six months in the new one, I was once again asked to offer my resignation.

In the state of New Hampshire, an employer does not need cause to fire an employee. But fortunately, if an employee is fired without cause, the employer is required to pay unemployment (I had already learned to manage on a fraction of my former income, and the unemployment was not too far from that fraction). On the other hand, I soon found out that the state agency had the power to interfere with my chances to work for *any* agency in New Hampshire.

If you choose to stand for what is right, don't for one minute think that it means you will win in this world.

I started once again to try and figure out where God wanted me to go. I did not want to return to engineering, and as I said, it had become apparent that returning to social services was also not going to happen.

That year we were homeschooling my daughter. Knowing that it would be difficult to find a position equal to my resumé, I decided to stay on unemployment and take an active part in her education. Then, near the end of my unemployment period, I received a job offer from a small manufacturing company in the area of Keene, New Hampshire. They were looking for an operations manager (it has been my experience that management is management).

While I dug into this new enterprise, I also began to give Bible studies in the area and speak at some of the local Seventh-day Adventist churches. This kindled a new fire in my soul. I was beginning to realize (again) that perhaps this was the direction in which God was leading me.

Years earlier, when I had graduated with my degree in religion from Atlantic Union College, I had actually spurned the idea of going into the ministry. Part of the difficulty at the time had been the fact that we were taking care of my father-in-law, who had become a quadriplegic (and eventually passed away, several years after I graduated).

But now those thoughts were returning. I asked my wife if she would consider my going into the ministry. She agreed that the timing was now better. I started to speak in as many churches as I could. Soon I found that I was going somewhere every weekend.

Chapter 40: Pastor Finally

While attending the birthday party of Pastor Nick, an old friend (in fact, the same pastor who had assisted me so long ago during my legal struggles with the Coast Guard), I spoke about my longing to go into the ministry. I said how I should have done it many years earlier.

Pastor Nick looked at me and smiled. He asked me to raise my right hand, then he asked me to raise my left hand. Looking me in the eye, he said, "You don't look dead to me!"

We both chuckled, then I quickly said, "But at fifty-five I'm too old to start over in the ministry."

He calmly said that Moses was eighty, so I had no room to talk. Then we discussed the best approach, and with his direction I prepared a resumé for some of the smaller conferences (though I had been an engineer the better part of my life, my undergraduate degree was actually a BA in religion with a master of science in management).

I received beautiful letters that basically said that my goals were high and *don't call us, we will call you*. I knew what they meant because I had written many such letters in my years in the corporate world! I was determined, however, to not give up.

My next approach was to corner the conference president and talk to him face-to-face. I did so at the Northern New England Conference of Seventh-day Adventists, only to be told once again that it probably wouldn't happen.

Then, after one particular phone call with the president while I sat in my car, he told me that, though he felt it was unlikely, if God was truly behind it, it would in fact happen.

As I hung up from that call I turned my car back on to return to work. The CD that I had in the player started to play the beginning of a song: "Hold on, hold on a little longer."

It is amazing how God can talk to us in different ways. He communicates to us through prayer, people, music, or situations. In that moment I felt this was exactly what He was doing, because what I didn't tell you is that I did not even have the CD player on when I first stopped the car!

I was sure that God was giving me just the encouragement I needed: to wait ... for the phone call that came one week later!

It was once more the president of the conference, asking if I would serve as interim pastor in both Keene, New Hampshire, and West Townsend, Vermont. I was told that I would receive a stipend for mileage. All I had to do was speak for the church services.

I asked if I was limited to just speaking. If the ministry was what God wanted for me, then I wanted to throw myself into His work. The president responded that I could do what I thought was necessary.

I had worked long hours for social services (it is not an 8 to 5 job). Likewise, as a manager in the corporate world, I had never worked just 8 to 5. Now was my opportunity to find out if I was up to the task of being a messenger for Jesus. After a few months, I realized that it was all I thought it would be and more! This was the direction in which Jesus had been pushing me.

Once again I approached the conference. I asked if there was some way that this work could be made full-time. Once again I was told that it probably would not happen, so I continued working my day job and doing pastoral work as my night job.

After helping one of the churches where I was interim to interview several potential pastors, one of the members asked me why they didn't make *me* the full-time pastor. I just smiled and responded that it was up to God. What I did not know then was that several members were busy writing to the conference.

In early October the small company where I worked decided to move their manufacturing to New York. I could not go there and continue with the church work I was doing, so they gave me a generous severance package that would carry me for thirty days. At the end of that time period, almost to the day, two strange things happened:

First, while I was at a prayer meeting for the little church in Vermont, some of the members came to me and expressed their excitement, because they had just heard that I had been hired full-time as their pastor. I had not been aware of this, so I told them that I would have to check and verify whether this had actually happened.

Then the next day (just as the severance money ended, I might note), I received a paycheck that was decidedly more than my travel stipend.

I called the conference office. They informed me that I had been hired full-time. They also said that I was going to pastor the Washington,

New Hampshire, church as well, giving me three churches total! Within three months, a fourth—the Drewsville church—was added to my district (you, reader, will be visiting Drewsville soon).

God's timing is always perfect. In retrospect, I see God directing my steps all my life. Had I realized this earlier (the true meaning of seeking first the kingdom of heaven), I would have avoided many two by fours and shots across my bow!

The biggest problem I had, and have, in common with most people is that I am willing to talk but less willing to listen. Prayer was never meant to be a one-way conversation. It is and has always been meant to be two-way! The sooner we realize this, the sooner we can climb the steps up which God is leading us!

CHAPTER 41: SEEING A MIRACLE

And whatever things you ask in prayer, believing, you will receive. (Matt. 21:22)

I have witnessed many miracles, some direct and some indirect. There was none more pronounced than the one I'm about to describe.

A family's son had been in a terrible accident. He had been struck by a drunk driver, and now he was in a coma. It was believed that he was beyond recovery. He was unresponsive; only being kept alive by the life-support system to which he was connected. The doctors were just waiting for the okay from the family to pull the plug. The parents asked if I would go with some of the elders and do an anointing.

I know that anointing is not a miracle cure. Its purpose is generally to pronounce blessing or help someone be at peace with a situation

Chapter 41: Seeing a Miracle

that they are facing. I debated whether this fit that purpose, but I agreed to go to University of Massachusetts Hospital and anoint the young boy.

Having been in a similar situation with my own family, I knew the struggle that they were going through. Perhaps I was thinking that the anointing would at least put the minds of the parents at ease. What happened was far more than I could have ever anticipated.

When we arrived at the hospital, the nurse in the boy's room was busy, so I explained what our purpose was and asked if we would be in her way. She told us that we could do whatever we needed to do, as there was literally no chance that this boy would ever recover or even be aware of what was happening.

Then I saw the young boy in the bed, connected to all the tubes, and my mind flashed back to when I was just twelve years old, and my grandfather lay in a hospital bed in a similar state.

I had always looked up to my grandfather. He was truly what they called a man's man! He was as big and broad as they come, and he was the captain of his own fishing vessel. And his ship was at sea more than it was home ... something else that I could relate to!

Because of the hard conditions and the heavy labor that fishermen endure, they age far too early ... and they wear that age on their faces and bodies. When my grandfather developed a constant cough, he wrote it off to the rough life that he had to live (which reminds me: I also have a lot of respect for the disciples of Jesus).

My grandmother tried to get him to have that cough checked, but he was always too busy; that is, until the government decided to close the fishing grounds for a few weeks. That meant that he *had* to stay in port. Thus, while my other grandfather (who worked on the same vessel) repaired nets, he went to the doctor to be checked out.

The doctor opted for exploratory surgery. When they opened him up, they discovered that he was riddled with Hodgkin's lymphoma. That's something else that I can relate to. I know the decisions he was facing.

I have been told that he received the highest level of radiation treatment yet administered at the time, as that type of treatment was then in its infancy. However, it seems that when cancer is exposed to the air, it's like throwing gas on a fire. Not long after the exploratory surgery, he lapsed into a coma.

My grandmother was there by his side every day reading Scripture; both to comfort herself and in the hope that he could hear what she was saying (I should add at this point that prior to this, my grandfather had showed no desire for religion; he felt it was for women, and he was too busy to give it much thought).

After quite a while, there came the day when he woke up. The shock almost did my grandmother in! He asked for the pastor, and when the pastor came, he gave his heart to the Lord!

It turned out that even while he lay in the coma, he had been aware during all those hours that my grandmother had been reading Scripture. He said that he had been praying to God to give him one more chance to make his peace. God could easily have granted my grandfather his peace without waking him up, but by doing so, God also received the glory He deserves.

My grandfather died two weeks after that point, but first he talked to each of his grandchildren and urged them not to wait. What he told me was that religion is for all, and delaying a decision is a foolish choice.

> *Just as I touched him and started to once again pray for God's blessing the whole room came alive!*

All of these thoughts and memories were running through my mind as I looked at this young boy, barely in his twenties, lying on a hospital bed.

We began the anointing as usual with a time in prayer. Then I placed a drop of oil on the boy's forehead. Just as I touched him and started to once again pray for God's blessing (as is the norm), the whole room came alive!

Alarms went off, and people rushed to our location. The young boy's eyes opened, and he turned his head to look at the elder and me. He was probably wondering what was happening. We realized that something major was taking place, so we stepped back and let the doctors do their thing.

The next day we were informed by the family that the boy had indeed awakened from the coma, and he was able to sit up in a chair. Within two more days, he was discharged and returned home. I would not have believed it possible had I not been there!

I know that God still does miracles. When we ask in prayer, believing, we receive.

CHAPTER 42: SPEAKING THE WORD

But when they deliver you up, do not worry about how or what you should speak. For it will be given to you in that hour what you should speak; for it is not you who speak, but the Spirit of your Father who speaks in you. (Matt. 10:19, 20)

I've always been fascinated by this verse. I used to wonder just how true it could be. It seemed like an excuse not to study the Bible.

This was all before I understood the concept of relationship. When you understand that our salvation is based on a relationship *with* Jesus, and not on just a knowledge *of* Jesus, it all starts to make sense. Having a relationship with Jesus is all about spending time in His Word on a daily basis.

Some new neighbors built a home just down the road from us. At first they were not warmly received in the neighborhood. This was due in part to their having nine children, all homeschooled, and in part due to their membership in a close, strict Catholic group.

We felt badly about the lack of acceptance of this family, so we made a concerted effort to befriend them. They were actually wonderful people, and the children were extremely well-behaved. It was not long before the younger children started to look to my wife and I as surrogate grandparents, and we also developed a wonderful relationship with the mother and father.

Because the group that this family belonged to did not readily accept outsiders, we were surprised when one Fourth of July we were invited to a celebration at their house. I decided to attend.

When I arrived the father of the family told me to go and have a seat beside the senior priest of the group. The priest was sitting in the front yard and appeared to be the center of attention. I went out, and as soon as I sat down, four more priests pulled their chairs into a circle around me.

This gave me a very awkward feeling, and I wondered what was up as they sat facing me. Then, one by one, they began to fire questions at me about my beliefs.

For every question, a Bible text immediately came to mind. For some time, I responded with Bible texts alone (to this day I am not sure where they all came from). After some fifteen minutes of this process, the senior priest raised his hand and all the questions stopped.

He then turned to me and asked if I believed that Jesus had come to this world to establish His church.

I knew where this was going because of the nature of their sect and very strict beliefs. Still, I do believe that Jesus came to this world to establish his church, so I answered, "Yes."

He then smiled and said that Peter was the rock of that first church.

I answered that Jesus had indeed called Peter "Cephas," which is translated, "a stone," from John chapter 1, verse 42. But I then quickly added that in Matthew chapter 21, Jesus had referred to Himself as the chief cornerstone, and that Peter himself had also referred to Jesus as the chief cornerstone in 1 Peter chapter 2.

At that point he frowned at me and repeated that Peter was the head of the first church.

I responded from the book of Acts, where it describes James as being the head of the first church in Jerusalem (like I said, to this day, I am not sure where all these texts came from or how I was able to recall them on the spot).

It was apparent that the priest was not happy with my comments. He declared that I was an independent thinker. The other priests then turned their chairs around and put their backs to me as an illustration that I was to be shunned.

I remember a later time when one fellow from this group came to my house and started to argue with me about the very same thing. But that time I began to argue back, and none of the answers that I had given before came to mind. I realized on that day that nothing is gained by arguing.

The obvious difference between the two incidents is that in the first case, God was getting the glory, while in the second, I was in a state of argument. We can accomplish little for the Lord in a state of argument. The purpose of the text that I began the story with is to let us know that when we are called to defend our faith, God must always receive the glory … and we must always defend in a spirit of love!

CHAPTER 43:
AGE VS MISSION

Therefore whoever confesses Me before men, him I will also confess before My Father who is in heaven. (Matt. 10:32)

Shortly after completing an evangelistic series (which I talk about in the next chapter), I learned of a gentleman in his nineties who was a member of the Drewsville Church and resided in a nursing home in Claremont. From what I understood, he had been very active in the church earlier in his life before being confined to the facility. I decided to visit him.

As I drove to see him, thoughts of my grandmother, who had been in the same plight, came to mind. Once she was moved into a care facility, she had deteriorated quickly; likely due to lack of contact with family and friends (this has a major effect on all of us).

Earlier in life she was always vigorously sharing her belief and her love for the Bible. My uncle once told me how several Jehovah's Witnesses had knocked on her door one fine day and offered Bible studies. She had readily accepted, on the condition that for every Bible study *they* presented, they would take a study from *her*. After several months those young Witnesses were baptized into the Seventh-day Adventist Church!

When I arrived in Claremont, I was taken to the old man's bedside. He was asleep, so I sat down and waited until he awoke. After about ten minutes, I heard him say, "Stop, mister!" Then his eyes opened, and he looked at me with surprise.

We had never met nor had I called ahead to mention that I would be coming, so I'm sure he had no idea who I was. But despite the lack of that small bit of information, he smiled and wished me a good day. Then he asked me who I was.

After introductions, he started to tell me how he was unsure why God continued to have him hang on. He made it known that he was ready to go to sleep; he felt there was nothing more that he could do.

I thought it must have been hard for him to have been so active, then confined to one location and unable to spread the Word as he had in the past.

Then he proceeded to tell me how he had studies going with two of the aides who attended to his care, and my sympathy was relieved! He asked if I had any literature with me.

I happened to have a few copies of *Desire of Ages,* so I went to my car to retrieve them. When I returned, he told me that he had plans for these books concerning a few of the other aides that were in the nursing home. And in fact, while I was there, several of the aides stopped in. They all had a smile and a happy word for this person they knew as a special man.

Before I left I asked to have a prayer with him. He asked if I would ask the Lord to reveal why he was still here.

I looked at him, then I looked at the books that he was already putting someone's name in. This man in his late nineties (I believe he was ninety-nine at the time) was doing more to spread God's Word than many of those half his age!

I quoted to him from Esther chapter 4, verse 14b: "Yet who knows whether you have come to the kingdom for *such* a time as this?"

We must always remember our primary mission in this world. We must not let it be buried under the day-to-day troubles that we deal with.

CHAPTER 44: EVANGELISTIC SERIES

And Jesus came and spoke to them, saying, "All authority has been given to Me in heaven and on earth. Go therefore and make disciples of all the nations, baptizing them in the name of the Father and of the Son and of the Holy Spirit, teaching them to observe all things that I have commanded you; and lo, I am with you always, *even* to the end of the age." (Matt. 28:18-20a)

There are yet many stories, but all things must come to a close; so I'll share two more accounts, then we'll wrap up and save the rest for another time.

As I recounted in "Pastor Finally," shortly after I was officially hired as a pastor, I was given two additional churches (on top of the two where I had already been serving as interim). One of these new churches, Drewsville, was scheduled for an evangelistic series in February 2006.

However, at the end of December, the evangelist contacted me. He was concerned that there was not sufficient time to do the pre-work necessary in another church and still have a series in my church in February. I suggested having the series at the Keene church instead, but the evangelist's first comment was that six months of pre-work was needed for an evangelistic series to be successful.

It's interesting that Jesus told us to go out and make disciples of all nations, but He didn't set time limits on the preparation necessary to bring people to Him. So after some discussion, it was decided to give it a try. We kept that coming February (just one-and-a-half months away) as our goal.

The first hitch was that we were unable to establish a site outside of the church for more than four meetings. It was felt that moving to the church too soon would drive people away, but once again we decided to proceed.

The second hitch came in the first week of January, when our personal ministries leader had a stroke. This shifted the effort to mobilize the church back to me.

Then the second week of January started off with my hospitalization for spinal meningitis. I was not released until the third week, and I was supposed to be on light duty only.

So there we were, with just a few days when the event could meet offsite, minimal leadership to mobilize it, and the series set to start in the beginning of February!

The devil will throw whatever he can into the pot to spoil the meal, but God is able to strain out the bad and retain the good! We held the first four meetings, and thirty-five people from the community were present by the end of those four days. The evangelist and the church members were skeptical that we would be able to shift locations without a large drop in attendance, but when we moved to the church, thirty-two of those who had started continued.

That did not mean the devil wasn't still working. One of those attending broke a leg and was unable to continue (but we were able to meet with her in her own home for ongoing Bible studies). Still, after twenty-six meetings, thirteen people had committed to the Lord to be baptized.

But the devil was not done. The morning of the baptism, something happened to the baptismal tank and the water had to be drained! During the church service, I could hear the tank refilling behind me. Then I realized that there was no warm water to add to the well water … it was 54 degrees!

As I stepped down into the baptismal, my mind went back to a story of the Washington, New Hampshire church. During the winter of 1865 (which was not just any winter but rather the fourth-coldest recorded in the town's history), twelve young people requested to be baptized after a series of meetings by James and Ellen White that took place at Christmastime. These young people, with their pastor, cut a hole in ice that was two feet thick in order to proceed with the baptism.

I knew in my mind that *that* water had been far colder than the water I was now stepping into, but that was cheap comfort. However, as the baptisms progressed, the water became warmer and warmer … at least in my mind it was so. Then again, cold is a state of mind!

There are times when we feel we have to accomplish certain things before God can do His work, but in reality there is nothing we need to accomplish before the Holy Spirit can touch the heart. Furthermore, the devil cannot stop what the Holy Spirit blesses!

Like I said, thirteen people gave their hearts to God during that series. We were reminded that you cannot underestimate the power of the Holy Spirit!

CHAPTER 45: TRUST

Trust in the Lord with all your heart, and lean not on your own understanding; in all your ways acknowledge Him, and He shall direct your paths. (Prov. 3:5, 6)

God's law and His entire character are based upon love. We in turn express love for Him by trusting His direction and accepting all He sends our way. This trust also extends between His children in ways we cannot begin to comprehend.

This story illustrates how trust in God allowed two people who had never met and did not know each other to trust each other … and thus save a life!

In my Coast Guard days, shortly after beginning one patrol, the ship received an emergency call from a tug boat off of Plum Island, Massachusetts. It had broken down, and its cargo, consisting of a barge full of crude oil, was adrift. The immediate danger was to the cargo and the New England shoreline. The tug had dropped anchor and wasn't going anywhere, but if that barge were to run aground and rupture, the environmental disaster would be enormous.

We were just off the coast of New Hampshire, so we were the closest response vessel. Our new captain was eager to show his prowess. Unfortunately, he neglected to assess the dangers to the tug.

Had he questioned their crew, he might have discovered that when they had cut the barge loose to save the disabled tug from being pulled under, they had lost communication with the man on that other ship. More importantly, the tow line was adrift as much as fifty yards away from the tug (with this bit of information, we could have avoided the disaster that would ensue).

As we approached the barge's location, a heavy fog bank wrapped itself around the coast. We could see nothing beyond a few feet. But we did have radar!

So since we were blind except electronically, the captain called for the manning of the combat information center (the CIC: a special room below the bridge). He didn't want any distractions from the lookout on the bridge. All active controls were shifted to CIC's command. My function, in such a scenario, was to man its radar.

The captain wanted to approach the barge and pull beside it (like a tug). The master chief suggested that this would not be wise, but the new captain, sure of his choice, moved forward.

Twenty yards from the barge, our whole ship shuddered and a huge explosion came from the fantail. In the same instant we stopped all forward movement! The captain quickly tried to reverse the propellers, thinking we had hit something.

What had actually happened was that we had found the drifting tow hawser! And by reversing the propellers, we melted the hawser onto the shaft and warped both of them. We would not be going anywhere but to a shipyard. Realizing our predicament, the master chief called to drop anchors both fore and aft! Now we completed the floating city.

We lowered a small boat of men who boarded the barge. They discovered that the man there needed immediate medical assistance. When the tow line had snapped back, it had rendered him unconscious. His wounds were deemed critical, so an emergency dispatch was made to the Coast Guard air station at Pease Air Base.

So as I watched on the radar, a helicopter lifted from the runway back at the base and climbed to 1,000 feet. I noticed that though the helicopter was raising straight up, the object on the radar representing it was shifting to the side. I marked the location at 500 feet and again at 1,000 feet. The triangle this created became an interesting equation as I calculated the shift. I then tried to calculate the progression and altitude as they headed our way (okay, so math geeks get their thrills creating equations! Trigonometry can be fun in a strange way).

As if the day had not been bad enough, the helicopter stopped. They announced that their radar had failed, so they were going to reverse course and return to base. Could we give them the course?

The crew on the barge said they were not sure how much longer the sailor there could hold on. If the helicopter left, he might surely die.

An alarm went off in my head. I asked to talk to the pilot directly.

Master Chief Jenkins, who had taken the con in the CIC, asked me what I was up to (he liked me and was curious as to where this was going).

I told him I thought I could direct the chopper until it was directly over the barge, then lower it to an altitude from which they could drop the basket to the deck.

Looking at my scratch pad and all the equations, the master chief shook his head and said, "Give it a shot."

I called the pilot and relayed my idea to him. There was silence for a minute. He responded by asking how I could possible do this. I told him of my little experiment, and stated that between it and prayer, this was possible (I know, prayer is not allowed on duty; it just slipped out).

After another few minutes of silence, he said, "Let's give it a go."

I did a quick calculation to figure his course. I told him to climb to 1,000 feet, because I had him at 800. Surprising me, he acknowledged that I was correct, then he went up.

"Now follow this course until I tell you to stop," I said and gave him instructions. Away he went.

I had marked the destination with a grease pencil on the screen. When he reached it, he stopped on my command. "Now you are 1,000 feet above the deck," I said. "Drop 800 feet." I recalculated and then asked how much line they had on the basket.

He said, "100 feet."

I figured the barge to be about 10 feet above the water, so I had him drop another 100 feet. From that spot they dropped the basket. It hit the deck about 80 feet below them. Not perfect, but darn close!

The wounded man was loaded in the basket and hoisted up to the chopper. As the pilot climbed back up to 1,000 feet, I gave him a course to return to the runway (where I had started my calculations). Once they were there, I told him to drop to 100 feet and then slowly continue to the ground. They landed right near the spot they had taken off from, and the wounded sailor made a full recovery.

Are you wondering what this has to do with the Bible text? Well, that is the rest of the story!

Flash forward four years to an isolated station in Alaska. A supply helicopter had landed at Cape Sarichef with supplies, but one of its rotors had cracked. The helicopter could not leave until parts arrived, so the pilot, a CWO, had come to the station and was killing time by sharing stories about his exploits.

One was about a mission he had flown off the coast of Massachusetts some four years earlier. He told how a crazy radar man had saved a wounded sailor with some strange calculations. He had even put the man in for a commendation, but it was squashed by the captain of the ship, who had been reprimanded and would be darned if someone else on his ship would profit from his error.

I told the CWO pilot that it had not been a radar man but a crazy ETN2! When he realized it was me, we had a great laugh. I then asked him whatever possessed him to try my scheme.

He told me it was only because I had mentioned prayer! He was himself a Christian; and since the radar operator was also a Christian, he was impressed to trust in God to keep it all together.

We can always put our trust in God, as He has promised to direct our steps. He will impress us to do what He wants us to do if we only listen. We need to develop ears attuned to God's voice. Talk to Him, but also know that communication implies a two-way discourse!

CHAPTER 46: KISS

And this is the testimony: that God has given us eternal life, and this life is in his Son. He who has the Son has life; he who does not have the Son of God does not have life. (1 John 5:11, 12)

This brings us full circle, as we come back to one of the first texts that I used and the one that is probably the most important to remember.

When I first finished fourteen weeks of basic electronics training, they proceeded into several more weeks of troubleshooting, utilizing the knowledge we had gained in the first fourteen.

On the first day of application, the teacher wrote on the board in front of the class one word: *KISS!* He then proceeded to tell us that the word he had just written was the key to all troubleshooting. He said that what it meant was, "Keep it simple, stupid!"

He went on to explain that the problem most people had with troubleshooting was that they overcomplicated the problem. "Try to break a problem down to its simplest form," he said. "In 99% of cases, you will find the solution without having to reengineer the equipment."

I have never forgotten his advice, and I have applied it to a hundred different things! The most important application has been the concept of salvation.

Many people want to overcomplicate the reality of the above verses, but the truth of the matter is that he who has the Son has life, and he who does not have the Son of God does not have life! It can't get any simpler than that.

Why do we have to make it so complex? Why does it have to be so difficult when it is not difficult? Having Jesus is all about relationship, not performance. Jesus tried to make this clear in John chapter 15 when He stated over and over again to abide in Him.

I'm going to close this book with a list. It starts with a passage that every Jewish person memorized as soon as they were old enough to retain language: "Hear, O Israel: The Lord our God, the Lord *is* one! You shall love the Lord your God with all your heart, with all your soul, and with all your strength" (Deut. 6:4, 5).

In the same chapter of Deuteronomy, we are then commanded to write this on our hearts, to teach this diligently to our children, and to talk of it when we sit in the house, when we walk by the way, when we lie down, and when we rise up. We are told to bind these truths as a sign on our hands and as frontlets between our eyes, and to write them on the doorpost of our houses and on our gates (Deut. 6:6-9)!

How much more explicit can God get than to tell us it is all about love, and love is all about relationship?

I'm going to leave this next series of texts for you to look up. If, after reading them, there is still any question in your mind that salvation is simple, I have closed with one last text which I have written out.

Luke 10:25-34
John 10:27-30
John 6:35-37
John 15:1-17
John 3:14-17
Matt. 6:31-34
Matt. 16:24-27
Matt. 19:25, 26

But of Him you are in Christ Jesus, who became for us wisdom from God—and righteousness and sanctification and redemption—that, as it is written, "He who glories, let him glory in the Lord." (1 Cor. 1:30, 31)

NOT the end but the beginning!

BIBLIOGRAPHY

White, Ellen G. *Desire of Ages*. Mountain View, CA: Pacific Press Publishing Association, 1898.

TEACH Services, Inc.
P U B L I S H I N G

We invite you to view the complete
selection of titles we publish at:
www.TEACHServices.com

We encourage you to write us
with your thoughts about this,
or any other book we publish at:
info@TEACHServices.com

TEACH Services' titles may be purchased in
bulk quantities for educational, fund-raising,
business, or promotional use.
bulksales@TEACHServices.com

Finally, if you are interested in seeing
your own book in print, please contact us at:
publishing@TEACHServices.com

We are happy to review your manuscript at no charge.

www.ingramcontent.com/pod-product-compliance
Lightning Source LLC
Chambersburg PA
CBHW071158160426
43196CB00011B/2124